W. O.

THE AUTOBIOGRAPHY OF
W. O. BENTLEY

(*Benjafield*)

W.O.

AN AUTOBIOGRAPHY

W. O. BENTLEY

HUTCHINSON OF LONDON

HUTCHINSON & Co. *(Publishers)* LTD
178–202 Great Portland Street, London, W.1

London Melbourne Sydney
Auckland Bombay Toronto
Johannesburg New York

★

First published 1958

*Set in eleven point Baskerville, two points
leaded, and printed in Great Britain
by The Anchor Press, Ltd.,
Tiptree, Essex*

ACKNOWLEDGEMENTS
AND AN APOLOGY

A number of people have been helpful in the writing of this book, jogging my memory, looking up dates and records and writing me letters, among whom I should especially like to thank R. A. Clarke, George Duller, Jack Dunfee, Clive Gallop, H. Kensington Moir, Hubert Pike, R. S. Witchell, my brothers, H. M. and A. H. Bentley, and my sister 'Poppy'. I am also grateful to R. A. Clarke for the loan of photographs.

I have, I think, been more fortunate than most in the members of my design staffs, and I should like to record my gratitude to F. T. Burgess and H. Varley who worked under me on the Bentley, to C. S. Sewell, who carried on their good work and helped with the Napier-Bentley, to S. S. Tresillian who worked on the V12 Lagonda and W. G. Watson and D. Bastow who worked on the 2½-litre Lagonda. The creation of any motor-car involves the close co-operation of a lot of people, and I wish it had been possible to include in this book the names of everyone else who helped with the aero engines and cars. I hope those who are not mentioned will forgive me, for I have not forgotten them.

W. O. B.

CONTENTS

ILLUSTRATIONS

AUTHOR'S NOTE

One or two people have showed some understandable alarm when I have told them that
I have written my autobiography, for they
know that I am about as proficient with a pen
as I am at making after-dinner speeches. But
I have always hastened to add (as I do now)
that I received help; or, more correctly, that
the book was largely written by Richard
Hough, who exchanged tape recordings and
worked closely with me for several months,
here and at his home, and met many of the
people with whom I worked in the old Bentley
Motors days. The responsibility for any merits
or deficiencies must therefore be shared equally
between us.

W. O. BENTLEY
Shamley Green

THE CHARM OF STEAM

THE motor car seemed to me a disagreeable vehicle. Perhaps I should have realized the vast potentialities of internal combustion and recognized from my nursery days that it was to be the impelling force in my life. But the fact must be recorded that the motor car struck my young, literal mind as a slow, inefficient, draughty and anti-social means of transport. Motor cars splashed people with mud, frightened horses, irritated dogs and were a frightful nuisance to everybody.

Before I rode in a motor car I had reached the susceptible age of sixteen, when it might be thought that the horseless carriage would have stimulated my natural curiosity if not my sense of romance. In fact my first ride was taken in a sort of omnibus. I sat in this vehicle on one of the two facing wooden-slatted benches behind the driver. It was a Daimler, with tube ignition—I must have been a little interested to have noticed that—and I remember the journey to Inverness as being thoroughly uncomfortable, the absence of any sort of protection, solid tyres, elementary springing and rough roads all contributing towards this. It was a wretched journey.

In 1904 I had no time at all for the motor car. It was the locomotive that held my devoted love. If I responded to that Daimler with no more than a flicker of interest, the sight of one of Patrick Stirling's eight-foot singles could move me profoundly. Ever since I had been conscious that the world was full of these great roaring masterpieces of engineering I had been fascinated and excited by them, and they filled my dreams and my ambitions. A few weeks after that short, unimpressive journey I was on my way to Doncaster from

King's Cross to fulfil these dreams and ambitions by becoming a premium apprentice at the Great Northern locomotive works.

The first fifteen years of my life were as calm, as lacking in crises and anxiety, as the following fifty years were to be eventful, anxious, often critical and nearly always exciting.

There were eleven of us—three girls, six boys, my mother and father—and an appropriate complement of servants in our Avenue Road house near Regent's Park in London, and I was the youngest by three years. The house survived until the 1940 bombing, when its numerous rambling rooms, solid walls, outhouses and stables were destroyed by a land-mine. The sight of its scarred ruins—all that remained of our noisy, happy home—made me rather sad when I saw them.

Our background was Yorkshire, direct paternally. But my maternal grandfather, Thomas Waterhouse, emigrated from Yorkshire to Australia in the early formative years of the colony, arriving in Adelaide a year or two after the city was founded, and promoted himself from the grocery trade to copper-mining and banking, and finally to philanthropy on a large scale. He returned to comfortable retirement in Hampstead and died there a few years later.

I was born at the usual disagreeably early hour on the morning of 16th September, 1888.

In early childhood my eight brothers and sisters seemed to loom over me in almost overwhelming profusion, and yet there was indulgence; possibly more than was good for me. I didn't resent it; except that I was always called Walter, I can recall no single childhood resentment. But I don't think I responded to this indulgent affection as warmly as my position as the Bentley baby demanded. In that fully populated, typically Victorian house I succeeded in being quiet and rather independent. I imagine myself at the age of five or six deeply involved in pulling something painstakingly to pieces, or equally painstakingly putting it together again, either in the big nursery we all shared or in my own bedroom.

My toys, of course, matched my interests, with a strong bias towards the mechanical. But there weren't many of them. No one had so many toys in the 1890s as they have today. But I did have a magnificent stationary steam-engine, given to me by an uncle, and heaven knows how many hours I spent with this treasured possession. Then there was a clockwork train set, probably crude by present-day standards, but I remember it as reliable and well made. I suppose shoddy toys must have been made sixty-five years ago, but I never saw any.

There were cricket and bicycles, later there were cameras, but in the final count it was the locomotive that reigned supreme. I can hardly remember our two nurses except their names, but my governess had a nephew who was an apprentice at Doncaster, reason enough for remembering her. This fact, plus my loyalty to Yorkshire and the Great Northern, settled Doncaster for me by the time I was eight, and I eventually landed up at the same digs as this envied, near-fabulous nephew. Walks with this governess nearly always tended to steer a course towards Loudoun Road, which at one point spanned the L.N.W.R., just outside the northern portals of the younger Stephenson's Primrose Hill tunnel. By careful timing we could catch the Scotsman getting into its stride as it bellowed out of the blackness and streamed past us towards Willesden. The station, now called West Hampstead, claimed hours and hours of my poor governess's time. Loudoun Road was in whistling distance one way from Avenue Road, Lord's a cricket-ball's throw the other way; but until the late 'nineties Loudoun Road had it every time.

Next door were the Thornhills, three boys and four girls as far as I remember, their ages parallel with ours. Geoffrey was the youngest and he was a train-fiend too. We spent hours together. Both our bedrooms were lined with copies of the *Railway Magazine*, the *Locomotive Magazine* and railway books, and on the walls were photographs and paintings of locomotives. We were both utterly single-minded, and the fact that he was as sternly loyal to the L.N.W.R. (his father was chief engineer on the civil side, so I suppose there was justice in this) as I was to the Great Northern, added spice to our relationship.

Around my little cell of busy enthusiasm the bigger Bentley world rotated on its more important, more adult axis. I was aware of it, of course, though it didn't impinge very seriously on my privacy; and I suppose it was aware of me, a certain amount of affection mixed with its curiosity. I think I struck my brothers and sisters as rather aloof, which, considering they were between three and twelve years older, seems strange.

I remember no unpleasantness, no unhappiness at Avenue Road. I was very fond of my father and mother, and they were devoted to each other. I don't think my father was very good at business, and he retired early. I must have inherited my shyness from my father. He was terribly shy, which caused him to seem unsociable and retiring to outsiders; with us he was naturally good-humoured, just and a good father, though I suppose you might call him a simple man. Anyway his philosophy was a simple one which, with a strong religious base, suffered misfortune and accepted fortune with equal calm; everything in life being pre-ordained. He was short and held himself very upright, and always wore a little moustache. Once he had sported an imperial, but it didn't last long. I have no doubt that he was suddenly struck with self-consciousness about it.

My mother had a great warm-hearted personality, with a strong will and determination and a complete certainty about what she wanted from life, and, what was more important to her, what she wanted from life for us. She was one of those people who leave a strong impression on everyone they meet and wherever they go, and she certainly had a great influence on all of us.

We had long, glorious family holidays, the first I can remember at Bridlington, then at scattered improbable places like Stevenage and villages in Suffolk, usually in rented vicarages or country houses. Wroxham on the Norfolk Broads was a favourite place. We had a boat as well as a house there and took turns to sleep in the boat. We also took turns to sail it, mine being notable for their brevity.

I think I was about fourteen when H.M., who was nearest to me in years, and I push-biked 130 miles to Wroxham. We did it in a day. It was my first experience of independent travel over a long distance and it left me with a lasting impression of achievement and of having fulfilled—on a very small scale— one of man's fundamental longings; one which has, I think, been implanted unusually strongly in me. In my bicycle I had the means to express this longing, and the fact that I usually made a dead set for the nearest railway line, to watch the trains, is by the way; it took me there, when I liked and almost as fast as I liked. I loved my bicycle.

They were quite advanced machines by the 'nineties, and bicycling was not the hazardous business then that it is now. Even in St. John's Wood there was only scattered horse traffic; it was a wonderfully safe and efficient way of getting about. The first cycle I rode had solid tyres. Then at the age of nine, by dint of furious saving and with a contribution from my mother, I managed to buy a second-hand one of my own. This I would take to pieces with a frequency and thoroughness that terrified my mother. She would find me sitting on the ground sur- rounded by cogs and bearings and wheels which she never expected me to be able to get together again. But I was slower and more careful than she gave me credit for; I can remember a few crises but I always managed the reassembly in the end.

When the inevitable day arrived, I found the prospect of going to school intimidating. I have sometimes been called a stoic—and because I have not suffered a succession of nervous breakdowns there must be some truth in this—and the idea of leaving home for prep school at the age of ten probably affected a lot of boys who had never before left home, or been to day school for that matter, a good deal worse than it affected

B

me. But I do remember being quite miserable when I was put on the school train with a great host of strange and extremely noisy boys, all of whom appeared to be on the most intimate terms with one another.

There were in fact sixty boys at Lambrook, trained to a severe standard of discipline by E. D. Mansfield, who had come from Clifton. In one form, and by one master especially, we were caned a great deal, and I had my proper share of it, mainly because I was so bad at lessons. I didn't like doing the things I didn't like and that was that. Besides this I was very slow at the lessons I did like, such as physics and chemistry, because I had to be satisfied that I understood the reason for every statement and argument. I was a great one for logical development, I had to see things through step by step, and if I missed one I had to go back to the beginning again. I had to know I was getting somewhere and I had to know why I was going, and this made for slow progress—and frequent canings.

For social success it was games that counted, of course, and for a while it looked as though my efforts were going to be equally disastrous on the rugger field. Games never came naturally to me and I really had to work hard and concentrate to achieve any sort of success. But cricket I enjoyed from the beginning. It had always been my first sport, Yorkshire has always been my first county and Wilfred Rhodes my first and greatest hero. I saw my first match at Lord's the summer before I went to school; Yorkshire were playing the M.C.C., and it was Rhodes's first match too.

To this day I take a lot of interest in the game and have over a hundred and fifty books on it. I'm only sorry it is taken so seriously now; the applause at the end of every maiden over, regardless of the quality of the bowling, strikes me as odd and undeserved. I like to do my own analyses of bowling on the number of balls bowled per wicket taken; every undistinguished maiden over deprives the fielding side's batsmen of valuable time for runs.

I've been lucky enough to see some of the epic matches of the past sixty years, and perhaps the greatest of all was the Oval Test Match against the Australians in 1902. I went there with my father on the last morning, when England, with 247 runs to get and three wickets down, early lost two more quick wickets. Then my hero Jessop came in, as always unperturbed by the situation. At once the match was transformed when 109 runs went up in the hour, and Jessop put England on the road to victory after slashing and stroking 104 in 75 minutes.

I think I have had more pure pleasure out of cricket than from almost anything else in life, and to get into the school eleven at Lambrook, go in first against a school at Reading and score 79 not out—as I did when I was twelve—gave me more satisfaction than anything that ever happened at Le Mans thirty years later. The other opener, incidentally, was S. S. Bonham-Carter, who later joined the Navy and (less shrimp-like than when I knew him) became a distinguished Admiral.

We had a wonderful gym at Lambrook. I enjoyed that, and I also won the school fives. Altogether I made out well enough in the fierce fight for games distinction, but it was a fight all the way; competition was red hot and a great deal depended on the result.

After a term or two I became accustomed to boarding-school and was able to accept it as a tiresome chore that took me away from my hobbies at home. But I never really got used to the sense of restriction, of being imprisoned, and above all I missed the freedom my bicycle gave me. At Lambrook we only went out for organized walks, and on Sunday to church, dressed in top-hats; and once a year to Ascot, a mile or two away, which sowed the seeds of my fundamental indifference to horse racing.

I don't remember any very close friends at Lambrook and I was probably as independent there as I had been at home. Nor do I remember any particular enemies, though I was horribly prone to getting into rows over bullying. That all started over two boys both of whom wore unorthodox clothes, and one of them had long curly hair, characteristics guaranteed to create trouble at a boys' school. Mass ragging soon developed in the playground against these two unfortunates in their early days, and this set my blood boiling. I went in with fists flailing, to the astonishment (but not I think discomfiture) of the attacking gang. I couldn't—nor can I to this day—tolerate any sort of bullying, physical or emotional. It is almost a passion with me, and one which has led me into many scraps, from prep school to middle age.

Apart from these episodes, and a few sporting highlights, Lambrook has not left me with many exciting memories. In spite of the discipline and the beatings it wasn't a formidable place. In fact we seemed to have spent a good deal of our brief spare time in such gentle pursuits as gardening our own little plots and, especially for me, photography. At the age of twelve I had been given a five-shilling box Brownie, which intrigued me vastly. I have always been devoted to gadgets, but photography soon left the 'gadgetry' class and became a real hobby. To take good photographs, to print and develop them myself in my own developing tank, was a constant challenge which I loved to accept. My first results were appalling, then I started to carry out my own research and experimentation and got better. I worked and worked away at that little Brownie and spent hours with it, becoming acutely depressed and angry when I took bad pictures and quietly excited when they turned out well. Oddly enough it was the master who was so severe and had been responsible for my canings who helped me most at school. A fellow enthusiast, he would show me some of the nicer points of the technique of printing. I still have some of those dim brown pictures—of cricket matches and buildings and boys—on which we worked together. In later years I think I must have wasted more money on photography than anything else, falling for that dangerous amateur's passion for ever more elaborate cameras and gadgets. I have now gone the full circle and my most recent purchase has provided me

with the simplest possible equipment—with which I am taking
the best photographs I have ever taken.

.   .   .   .   .

I suppose I was lucky to get to Clifton at all. My academic
standard was still abysmal when my time at Lambrook was up,
and I didn't deserve a place. But because my five brothers
had all been there I suppose they felt they couldn't very well
exclude the last Bentley. So in 1902 'the Bun' (my shape and
my two black eyes got me that name) followed the others into
Tait's house.

H.M. was second in command at Tait's at Clifton when I
went there in the autumn, and the three years between us
assumed the proportions of a vast gulf. In fact I saw very little
of him, though before I arrived he warned me about the
dining-hall boxing, a traditional public school endurance test
in which new boys were pitted against one another. 'A deuce
of a lot depends on how you make out,' he told me, 'so give it
all you've got.'

I practised like a fiend at the end of the holidays, so that
when I came up against a formidable boy called Murray, for
the bout in front of all the house, I was less depressed about my
hopes than perhaps I should have been. I went at him like a
demented monkey, energy and fanatical determination making
up for any lack of finesse.

It did the trick and I beat him—for the first and last time.
I often boxed with him afterwards, but never got the better of
him again.

Tait's was a converted private house in College Road,
overlooking the playing fields. I think Clifton was a good school
at that time, as it is today; but my life there followed a similar
undistinguished pattern to that at Lambrook. I hated nearly
all the lessons, except chemistry and physics, at which I was
quite good; but I seem to remember that the masters were
either more tolerant or more resigned. Anyway I didn't get
into so many rows, and on one epic occasion I actually got a

'Star' at chemistry. I again fought my way to a reasonable standard at most games, enjoying particularly the agility and concentration that fives demands. I threw myself into the rugger with sufficient enthusiasm to break my collar-bone, and I think both wrists. Cross-country running suited my temperament better than sprinting. It was a manageable sort of challenge that I enjoyed, and the technique could be worked out to a slowly developing formula.

But above all, of course, it was the cricket I enjoyed most at Clifton. I worked like a Trojan at cricket and got into the house team in my second year—not for my bowling, though I did bowl three expensive overs, nor for my batting, described in the house records as 'showing some powers of defence', but for my fielding. I was no good in the outfield, where I think I must have lost my nerve or become self-conscious waiting for the ball to arrive. But I was very good in the slips. I scored only five runs in the summer of 1904, batting on one great occasion for one hour for one run, but I caught out quite a few people and stopped enough balls to qualify for the report: 'a good field'. My second year in the team was a little less insignificant and I was opening bat—'a very consistent batsman, who watches the ball well'. I scored the second highest total of runs in the house, caught more catches than anyone else and actually took a few wickets.

I left Clifton early—at sixteen—to go to Doncaster, and never got out of the third form. I enjoyed my three years there well enough and made some good friends, like the little one-eyed Irishman Macnamara, and R. S. Witchell, now a director of E.N.V. gears, with whom I came into friendly contact again at Brooklands and at hill-climbs in the years before the war, in the R.N.A.S. during hostilities and finally, of course, as works manager at Bentley Motors. Roy Fedden was also there, senior to me; he was later to become a distinguished designer, first with Straker-Squire and then with Bristol on aero engines.

It was during those last holidays in the summer of 1905 that I went up to stay at a farm in Scotland where one of my brothers was training for an agricultural career, and it was then that I made my first acquaintanceship with that tube-ignition Daimler bus. Its impact, as I have said, was negligible at the time, except in terms of mild discomfort. It was still locomotives for me—with all my heart and all my enthusiasm. At Doncaster I would have my fill of these entrancing great beasts!

2

REALITIES ARE FACED

ONE alarum clock wasn't enough; it took two to get me out of bed at a quarter past five, and a cup of hot Bovril to bring me to consciousness. I then groped my way downstairs, lit the lamp of my bicycle, and wheeled it outside. It was pitch dark and bitterly cold when I mounted and pedalled off down Netherhall Road. There was a mile and a half to go across Doncaster to the Plant and I was no longer half asleep when I left my bicycle and walked over the railway bridge and in through the gates, my ears numb, my eyes running with tears.

To be even thirty seconds late was an unforgivable crime. The Doncaster regime really was a tough one and you had to be a devoted disciple to survive it. The first session was from 6 to 8.15 a.m., when there was a break for breakfast; then a four-hour stretch to one o'clock, and the final one from 2 to 5.30 p.m. Including half Saturdays it was only just short of a sixty-hour week, and there was no slacking, no knocking off for cups of tea and gossips. It was hard going every day and the timekeeping and discipline were to military standards.

On our first morning the new premium apprentices started the day with a brief to-the-point lecture on what was going to happen to us, given by a little nondescript man with a drooping moustache. To utter even the curt words of welcome appeared to pain him, and he seemed relieved to pass us over, raw, bewildered and thoroughly intimidated, to the first foreman, Treece. From him we received an equally chilly reception and were impressed with the standards of discipline expected of us. 'At the Plant, six o'clock *means* six o'clock,' he told us.

The formidable Growcock, under whom we were to serve

directly, seemed at first, through my seventeen-year-old eyes, to be more a sergeant-major than an under-foreman, and the two- and three-year apprentices like battle-scarred old campaigners, worldly, knowledgeable and rather frightening. At first I hardly dared to open my mouth when they were around.

The purpose of this alarming reception became clear only after some time, when I could look back at it objectively. To the foremen premium apprentices were mostly 'softies', gently nurtured beings from well-to-do homes. That there would be some material worth developing from among them was a certainty; the difficulty was to discover it, and, to save everybody's time, this must be done as quickly as possible. It was rather like the ancient tribal custom of sorting out the potential warriors from the male youths. The first weeks at the Plant were a testing time; those who were determined, keen and tough enough, survived the trial. Until they had, nothing was taken on trust.

It was no use pretending that there wasn't a barrier between the apprentices—sons of men who had lived all their working life on the Great Northern, bred and reared on locomotives—and the premium apprentices. The apprentices were paid five shillings a week from the day they started; premium apprentices paid their way in, a £75 premium for five years' slogging, though we did get this back in wages. I was ragged for my southern accent, even ribbed for being a snob, and there was plenty of horse-play. How you responded was watched carefully; if you came through—and just to be imitative wasn't good enough—the barrier dissolved and that was that.

Later, as a veteran, I had to help others through these tough early days. One of them was Gordon England, one of the earliest glider pilots, who became a big noise in the motor business. I had a lot to do with him in the Bentley Motors days, when the Doncaster period provided a strong link between us.

Once you were through and accepted you had only begun your lesson in human relations. Later I began to understand not only how to get on with the working man—that's not difficult—but also his mind: his pride, his conscientiousness, his loyalty, his attitude to life and his generosity. I've never met a group of men so generous as the apprentices and men at the Plant. The time and trouble they took to help you over a problem that was holding you up was sometimes overwhelming; it seemed almost a point of honour that they should unravel it for you.

Doncaster had lived by trains for fifty years. There was very little else there but the construction and maintenance works; there were no coal mines huddled round the little town then, and almost everyone was connected with the Great Northern in one way or another. The main road crossed the line in the middle of the town, and that caused no one any trouble. Doncaster had been the birthplace of Edmund Denison, first Chairman of the Great Northern, and it was he who had been responsible for setting up the big Plant there in 1853, incidentally bringing prosperity and a substantial increase in population to the town. He had tried to persuade his shareholders to pay for a church and school for his workmen, an uncharacteristic piece of misjudgement. Irate Victorians threw out his plan for the £8,000 church, and only allowed him his school with the utmost reluctance. It may not have been a very pretty place—railway towns rarely are—but I liked it, and there was pleasant country within easy bicycling distance.

The hierarchy at Doncaster in 1905 was tremendously impressive. There, in real life, as distant and awe-inspiring as stars to a dramatic student, but working in the same Plant and from time to time even allowing themselves to be seen, were some of the great heroes of my boyhood. As locomotive superintendent, of course, there was Henry A. Ivatt, who had taken over this post from Patrick Stirling ten years before. Ivatt had been responsible for the first Atlantic-type locomotives to be built in this country; they marked a dramatic departure from Stirling's eight-foot and seven-foot-six Singles, and were the linking design between the nineteenth-century express locomotive and the larger and more powerful superheated engines which were soon going to be needed on main lines.

Ivatt, I think, earned about £3,500 p.a. He was a tall, thin, very quiet man, much respected but not much liked because of his severity. I don't regard him now as a great designer; his main quality was his awareness of his own limitations, and because of this he knew he could not afford to make a mistake. Ivatt could never have survived a failure, and he never had one. This was in the strongest possible contrast to Nigel Gresley, then at twenty-nine already superintendent of the Carriage and Wagon works and due soon to succeed Ivatt. Gresley made many mistakes, but they were the mistakes of a genius and an original creator. Ivatt could never have produced the series of Gresley record-breaking Pacifics, which culminated in *Mallard's* 126 m.p.h. run in 1938.

Also under Ivatt were F. Wintour, the works manager, and O. V. Bulleid, his personal assistant, who was to achieve a fame almost equal to Gresley's as head of the Southern Railway's locomotive department.

Among the premium apprentices I had some real friends. There was Pat Macguire, a distinctive six-foot-sixer, who made himself even more prominent by always being in the wrong place at the wrong time in the Plant, and A. H. Peppercorn (of clerical stock like so many railwaymen), who many years later became chief of the locomotive department.

I had no cause to complain about my contemporaries; I got on well with the foreman now; I admired, even hero-worshipped, the aristocrats of the Plant. I had only one great sorrow and disappointment, made worse by its complete unexpectedness. Week after week, month after month went by, and I never even saw, let alone worked on, a locomotive. The only time I could catch a glimpse of one was when I sneaked out of the shop when the foreman wasn't looking—usually on the early morning shift—and poked around the erecting shops. For close-ups of my beloved engines, with all their grace, their sense of power, their speed and sound and movement that had made me their devoted slave for ten years or more, I should have done better to spend the day at Doncaster level-crossing. A year and a half passed before I got my hands on a locomotive. That was a bitter pill to swallow.

My first fitting work was on connecting rods in a shop at the far end of the top turnery, comparatively unskilled 'apprentice' labour. We had to put the radii and polish on the H sections, chipping away by hand at the sharp corners, trying to form an even cut of a quarter of an inch right along the eight corners of the H section without breaking the chip. It sounds tedious, but I found it fascinating. Afterwards the whole rod was filed up and the corners made into an even radius. All this exhausting and noisy work was done under the single (but eagle) eye of the charge hand, a fellow called Heap, who was all right if you did your best. His opposite number in the valve-motion part of the shop, Jack Bramley, was a wonderful and charming old man, well read, thoughtful, with a fine philosophy and a balanced view of life. I learnt a lot from him. I have another happy memory of his part of the works; my bench was against the window, and below was the main line, busy with 251 class Atlantics and sometimes one of the two surviving Stirling Singles.

It was a great advance to get into the foundry. There was something fundamental and creative about the foundry, with its huge cupolas, its heat and sand, and the sudden excitement when the delicate and highly skilled business of casting cylinders was taking place, a vivid, searing waterfall of molten metal. We worked on safe, simple stuff at first, things like maximum weight notices for goods wagons and carriage luggage-rack brackets. The birth from the furnaces of even these humdrum objects gave me enormous satisfaction, and I began to feel I was getting to the heart of things.

Gradually we moved around the Plant, until we got into the engine-erecting shop. This was a red-letter day I'll never forget. Here were all the bits and pieces we had been working on, filing and polishing, chiselling and casting over the past months, like old friends seen suddenly in a new and more appropriate environment. To raise the morale of munition workers during the war, I believe they were sometimes taken to an airfield or Army depot, and there, to their delighted surprise, they would be shown little bolts or sprockets, tiny and apparently meaningless metal panels which they had been turning out by the hundreds of thousands, and which were now seen actually to have a purpose as an integral part of a tank or aeroplane. There was nothing wrong with my morale when I started work in the erecting shop; but it was a pleasantly cheering experience.

You had to be fit and muscular to stand up to the work there. To fit up, by hand, slide bars on which the crossheads ran, making them bear evenly along their whole length by filing the packing pieces at each end, called for brute strength as well as skill. But for sheer filth combined with hard work there was nothing to match taking a blast pipe out of a locomotive in the engine-repair shop. The blast pipe, a sort of exhaust pipe, directs the used steam up the chimney, and the flange at its base is secured by a series of nuts and studs which are always so corroded that they have to be split with a hammer and chisel. Everything is so awkwardly placed that every blind blow brings a fall of soot into your face, and every tenth blow lands on your hand.

The underside of a car after a few thousand miles is as hygienic as an operating theatre compared with a locomotive in for overhaul. The wonderful mixture of congealed grease, oil, mud and dust has to be seen to be believed. It sometimes took me ten minutes to scrape away the filth concealing the nuts I was looking for. It took even longer to scrape the accumulated filth of a day's work off my hands, arms and face.

This problem of dirt—a thing the layman is inclined to forget—and the fatigue from a ten-hour day in the Plant just about settled the matter of evening entertainment. At Doncaster it hardly existed. At half past five I bicycled home, again in the dark in winter, to my digs with the Creaser sisters, the dear couple who looked after me so wonderfully well. After the prolonged business of cleaning and changing, I came down to a high tea—great spreads of chicken or pork pies or thick steaks, man's food for a ravenous young man. Then I might meet a friend or two, and as they were all quite as single-minded as I, we usually ended up on Doncaster platform talking shop.

I knew and liked as well as anyone there a fellow called G. C. Gowlland. He was an Army man from Woolwich on a course at the Plant for a few months. He was a terrific rugger player, had played for Scotland and London Scottish as well as the Army, and at Doncaster he was equally keen on keeping fit as getting through his course. He soon had me at it too.

'Shovelling's about the quickest way of keeping the muscles in trim,' I suggested one day. 'Good training for the footplate too.'

He jumped at the idea, and the next morning we were in the foundry, offering to stoke the cupola. The men there were always delighted to see us; they would generously hand over their shovels and be equally generous with their advice on the correct mixture of pig-iron and coke to throw in.

I still haven't heard of a better weight-reducer than stoking a cupola for an hour or two. Holding suitcases out at arms'-length in the train to London was another little self-imposed trial we endured.

There were more peaceful occasions with my Pathé gramo-phone. I fell for this in Clark's shop window in Doncaster and decided I had to have it. It was a very good machine, one of the early ones with a sapphire in the sound-box which elimi-nated the chore of changing needles. For the Pathé I accumu-lated quite a collection of records, ballet music and Faust mostly, and I reckon I got my money's worth from it. Music has always given me a lot of pleasure in spite of my technical ignorance. Rachmaninoff, Grieg, Tchaikovsky, Chopin; Layton and Johnstone, Tauber, Jean Sablon—my taste is catholic, but I do have my dislikes too!

On most Saturdays Gowlland and I made a dash for our digs at twelve o'clock, cleaned and changed and made the 1.03 London train with a few seconds to spare. Our special privilege tickets cost us only a few shillings and we were in Town for tea. Much as I loved my work, it was a relief to get back to the clean comfort of Avenue Road and the family, and the gaiety and glitter of the Empire or the Palace with old friends had their charm after the severity and austerity of Doncaster. The 8.45 from King's Cross on Sunday evening brought me back, and it was some time after midnight when I walked out of the station and set off for Netherhall Road. I can still remember the sound of the church clocks chiming above the silent streets and the smell of the Don wafting all over the town.

By the beginning of 1909 I was ready for the footplate. Through all my childhood years, through prep school and Clifton, through three and a half years of sweat and dirt and grinding work at Doncaster, the burning ambition to get on to a locomotive's footplate had remained with me. You could call it, I suppose, my ultimate physical ambition, equal and parallel to the more intellectual ambition to design locomotives. By 1909 I was one of Ivatt's pupils, and among the privileges this brought was footplate experience as second fireman.

Until the summer of my first year at Doncaster, premium apprentices often went as first firemen on the footplate. In the middle of September that year I had seen off from the station the York train, with premium apprentice Talbot as fireman. With Driver Fleetwood, he had then fired the 6.50 York to Peterborough, where the pair had taken over the semi-fast King's Cross–Edinburgh mail train, No. 276 Atlantic. This train, which was due to stop at Grantham, came fast out of Stoke tunnel south of the town, ignored the distant Caution signal, and came pounding through the station and past the red light at the north signal-box. Fleetwood and Talbot, who both knew the line well and were thoroughly steady characters, were last seen, one on either side of the footplate, looking

ahead; though other and less reliable eye-witnesses claimed to
have seen them struggling together on the footplate as if
Fleetwood had had a fit and Talbot was trying to minister to
him.

At the junction north of the station, where the points were
set against it, the engine left the rails, broke from the train and
was almost destroyed. It was a miracle that only ten others
were killed in the burning wreckage the Atlantic trailed
behind it.

This disaster made a tremendous impact on us at Doncaster,
of course. More experienced men than we argued hotly (and as
fruitlessly) on the cause of it. Even the Board of Trade enquiry
didn't settle the matter, and the Grantham crash remains one
of the greatest railway mysteries. The one positive result it had
was to prohibit premium apprentices from the footplate except
as second firemen.

It was decided after all that my footplate experience should
be taken at King's Cross, so I left Doncaster, with many
regrets, and came south to London to work in the running
sheds, and my two worlds were suddenly merged into one. For
four years they had been quite separate: the harsh, rough,
dirty, practical and classless world at the Plant; and the
comfort, gaiety and sociability of my Regent's Park life. Seen
from Doncaster, Avenue Road often seemed as unreal as the
overalled figure in the shops appeared when I was on leave in
London. I had not realized how strong the contrast had been
until it ceased to exist. At around six o'clock a filthy apparition
would bicycle up the short gravel drive of the Bentley home and
disappear inside to make himself fit for human company.
When the weather was bad and I didn't use my bicycle, I
crammed into the rush-hour Tube with my fellow commuters;
it was particularly good fun to watch the varied reaction of the
people who recognized me—or pretended they didn't.

Work at King's Cross was about the filthiest I ever got
involved in during my apprenticeship. Routine maintenance
was carried out in the running sheds, more serious overhauls

'The Bun'
1900—on the London–Cambridge
road

Lieutenant Bentley, R.N.V.R.
1916—aero engines for the
Admiralty

1909: the Rex
'Speed was beginning to get a
grip on me'

1914: D.F.P.
In the Tourist Trophy
with Leroux

Camel fighters, powered by B.R.1s, lined up at Braydunes, near Dunkerque

The B.R.2 or Bentley Rotary

and repainting being done at Doncaster. Examining fireboxes
not only made you filthy, but roasted you as well. Fireboxes
take a long time to cool down, too long to wait before the job
has to be done.

My first footplate work was as second fireman on local
goods trains, but I wouldn't have cared if it had been local
shunting. This was the beginning of one of the fullest and
happiest years of my life, and by the time I had worked up
through local passenger trains to main-line expresses I was in
my seventh heaven.

It is not often that childhood dreams mature into reality;
it is rarer still for there to be no disappointment or disillusion
when they do. I realize now how lucky I was that the sensation
of being on the footplate of a Great Northern Atlantic, heading
an express north out of London, was more thrilling and
wonderful than I had ever thought it could have been. I was
fascinated by the feeling of power as we pulled out of King's
Cross, up the steep gradients and tunnels of north London, up
the steady grind for another eleven miles to Potter's Bar, and
by the sudden irresistible surge of acceleration when the track
levelled off and fell away. There is nothing I know to compare
with the sensation of rushing through the night without lights
and with that soothing mechanical rhythm beating away continuously, even leading to a dangerous tendency to surrender
to the power quivering beneath the steel floor. And then the
signals flash into view, your absolute guide and master, and
from time to time the lights of a town, the searing white flash
of a station—and back into darkness.

My longest day was London to Leeds and back, on the
return journey doing Wakefield to King's Cross non-stop for
175 miles. This was a total day's run of 400 miles, entailing a
consumption of about seven tons of coal, every pound of it to
be shovelled. Not a bad day's exercise.

All this was wonderful for keeping fit, and I don't think I've
ever been so healthy in my life on all that fresh air and cold tea.
Firing a locomotive isn't just a matter of throwing shovelfuls of

C

coal into the box when the fire begins to look low. It would have taken me years to master the art, but I did learn something about keeping the pressure just right, anticipating requirements before coming, say, to a long up gradient, about dealing with poor coal, a dirty boiler, injector troubles and so on. I learnt a little about the art of driving too, but only a little, for it requires really uncommon skill. I have been on the footplate out of King's Cross in wet weather and with a heavy load when, in the smoke-laden blackness of the tunnels, the wheels have started to slip and, unless I actually leant out to feel the tunnel wall, there was no way of telling whether those 300 tons under the driver's care were moving backwards or forwards.

Oddly enough—and tragically too—this was how Cecil Kimber of M.G.s was killed. The train on which he was a passenger came slipping backwards out of the tunnel and his coach fouled the catch-points and upset. No one else was even hurt, I believe. I have worried about this wheel-slip in tunnels off and on ever since it first happened to me nearly fifty years ago and have tried to persuade the authorities to do something about it. The answer—a ratchet, perhaps, on the trailing wheels attached to an indicator in the cab—would be so simple, but the danger remains today.

• • • • •

Summer 1910. I had been working hard for five years. I was nearly twenty-two, my apprenticeship completed. It was a moment to take stock and reach a few conclusions about my future.

I wasn't at all sure that I liked what I saw ahead of me. Locomotives, as always, were nearest to my heart; familiarity had—if possible—improved relations between us. But, materially, what did they offer me? A job as a fitter, or at best the post of assistant to the assistant of the locomotive superintendent at King's Cross, with a maximum salary of £250 p.a. There were too few plum jobs, too long a waiting list for them when their present holders retired. And, like most young men of twenty-two, the material things of life interested me: gadgets, if you like, motor bicycles, some comforts and most of all the freedom from worry.

Suddenly, to my dismay, I realized that the railway was not going to be able to meet my wishes. Which way, then, was I going to turn? Over the past year or two, through my motor-cycle racing and other competition work (of which more later) I had at last become keenly aware of the internal combustion engine. A lot had happened since that trip in the Daimler up in Scotland. What had then seemed to me a tiresome and unreliable piece of machinery was now something to be reckoned with. The i.c. engine was carrying more and more people about the world, faster and more efficiently. It had even whisked a few people over the Channel. Internal combustion had to be taken seriously.

E. M. P. Boileau, who was on the staff of *The Autocar*, was an old friend of mine. Of all the people I knew he was obviously the best person to write to. He knew the motor business inside out. I suppose you can say that the letter I wrote him was quite a significant, even an important, one. Anyway, its results were important to me.

3

THE LURE OF SPEED

A LOT of people don't like motor bicycles, looking at them as I looked at the early cars as noisy, draughty and anti-social, and for the benefit of these and for people who are simply bored by them, all my motor bicycling—what you can call my 'two-wheel memoirs'—is concentrated in this chapter, which the reader can easily skip if he feels like it.

We have to go back a few years now, back to 1906 and to those somewhat rugged days at Doncaster. I have already mentioned my love for travelling and for covering great distances independently. One of the things I have always enjoyed most in life is to get out my maps (of which I have an enormous collection) and plot out a journey, imagining what the roads and the towns and villages are like, and then to carry out my itinerary. I don't think my delight in planned travel is unusual; certainly the excitement has not faded with the passing years, and remains with me as strongly as ever today.

At Doncaster the opportunities for travelling came rarely enough, but then one day I got hold of a copy of a magazine called *Motor Cycle*, and from its pages a wonderfully exciting new world opened up. A push-bike, it seemed, need not always be pushed; it could carry you along under the power of its engine, which helped you up the hills and allowed you to travel two or three times the distance in the same time. Neither the engine nor the additional speed it would give appealed in the least to me at first, the power striking me just as a very sensible means of exploiting an already admirable means of transport.

36

I thought about this motor bicycling for a time, and the more I thought the more I liked the idea. I bought and read more copies of *Motor Cycle*. Then, on one week-end leave in London, I went along to the nearest cycle shop, E. T. Morris's in the Finchley Road, where there were a lot of new and second-hand machines, both pedal and motorized. The one within my price range that I fancied the most was a 3-h.p. Quadrant, a belt-drive affair with a surface carburettor[1] and single-speed transmission. It must have been at least third- or fourth-hand for its registration number was an early one, A4667, and it had clearly seen a few years' service. Again after more thought and after discussing it with the family, I took the plunge, and came back to Avenue Road on it one evening, my self-consciousness changing to possessive pride when my brothers came out and looked over the machine admiringly and, I thought, even enviously. That little Quadrant was the first mechanically propelled vehicle any Bentley had ever owned, and I suppose it deserved this attention, just as in later years it had a lot to answer for.

Before long A.W. had a Triumph and H.M. a Quadrant like mine, and we were going out at week-ends together, comparing notes and religiously reading page by page the weekly *Motor Cycle*. For a brief period motor cycles ruled our lives. I remember being envious of the Triumph's magneto and mechanically operated inlet valve, so obviously the engineering of that somewhat crude engine soon began to interest me. I have never been able to use any piece of machinery for long without having to pull it to pieces to see how it works.

The romantically inclined A.W., on the other hand, didn't care a scrap about what made the wheels go round, and it was just as characteristic of him that he should learn about—and become fascinated by—a record which has alas now become extinct: the End-to-End.

---

[1] Many unkind things have been said about the surface carburettor, and it was a little tricky. But it was also very economical and worked well so long as you never let in more petrol by the needle valve than you could possibly use.

'You can't go much farther than that, can you?' I remember him saying, which is true of Great Britain, but as a practical proposition an attack on the record was quite absurd for someone who hadn't the least idea whether a cylinder worked inside a piston, or vice versa.

'You're not really thinking of tackling it?' asked H.M.; and was informed that of course he was.

It was also characteristic of A.W. that he should not only try but succeed, setting about the operation with the casual ease and transparent enjoyment that we loved in him. He set off from John O' Groats, driving a quite reliable machine but with the crudest of lighting day and night over macadamed or dirt roads that were almost unsignposted, and arrived at Land's End tired but in comfortable time to take the record. A year or two later he took the End-to-End record for side-cars, with H.M. this time, equally soundly. Both were remarkable achievements which would not have been possible without an equally remarkable element of luck.

I took my Quadrant back to Doncaster by rail and used it there for getting about the town, continuing to take the Great Northern home at week-ends, until it occurred to me one day to do the journey by road. This may sound commonplace enough, but it was a proposition to be considered carefully in 1906, with a machine with a top speed of less than 35 m.p.h., and the Great North Road less great and an even more second-rate highway than it is today. Anyway it was unusual enough to cause something of a sensation when I turned up at home, covered in dust and very tired, at nine o'clock one Saturday evening.

All this led naturally to the three of us joining the appropriate motor-cycling clubs, the Auto Cycle Union, the Motor Cycling Club and the North-West London Club, and taking part in their events. In fact we became rather ambitious, and A.W. even suggested that he and I should go in for the London–Edinburgh Trial. We must have been mad to consider it, for this was a major event in the calendar, supported by works'

teams and professional drivers. However, A.W.'s infectious
enthusiasm won the day as usual, and I found myself spending
week-ends preparing our machines.

A.W., of course, went right through without any mechanical
troubles and got a Gold Medal. As far as I was concerned,
things went well enough until Newcastle, though I had
arrived at each control only in the nick of time, which left
me dependent for refreshment on the chocolate and apples
and sandwiches I had in my pocket—and because of my
meagre power I had had to pedal up every hill. I was just about
all in when my rear tyre went flat somewhere around Morpeth,
and I was ready to give up. But a good Samaritan in the shape
of a fellow called Baddeley of the Newcastle club stopped and
gave me a hand, so I was able to stagger on until I was actually
in sight of Edinburgh—when my engine went dead. It was the
wire to the contact-breaker this time. It had broken, and it was
so tucked away that it was a major operation even to get at it.
But I managed to mend it somehow, and tore off to arrive at
the last control just in time. It was my first Gold Medal, and
the hardest-earned of them all.

I got my moneys' worth out of that Quadrant all right. I
don't remember what mileage I covered, but it included a tour
of Scotland with A.W. and H.M. As soon as I could afford it I
exchanged it for something better, and the next machine was a
one-off made specially for me by the Quadrant hill-climb
specialist, L. W. Bellinger, from a $3\frac{1}{2}$-h.p. engine, a lighter
frame and other bits. It worked very well, but by 1908 I was
converted to Rcxs, which were no more reliable but much
faster. The first was a 5-h.p. twin, an advanced machine with a
particularly good frame design. Being hand-built Rexs varied a
great deal, and you could be landed with a very bad one. I
was lucky; mine was a good one, I had enormous fun with it,
and it brought me Gold Medals in the London–Plymouth–
London and Lands End-and-back Trials.

The following year it was a $3\frac{1}{2}$-h.p. Speed Model Rex,
which was so fast that I got the wild idea that I might stand a

chance in racing. Speed, you see, was beginning to get a grip on me. To the gentle charm of assisted propulsion on two wheels had been added the exhilaration and effortlessness of fast movement along the roads, which you can only appreciate to the full on a motor bicycle. Speed, as we all know, has a strong cumulative factor, and in no time at all I was experimenting with the rather unresponsive Quadrants and later the Rexs to try to obtain more m.p.h. When I was successful I derived enormous satisfaction from this mild tuning; and as a natural corollary when I thought seriously about speed events I tried to perfect in the same way my driving, and especially my cornering. Motor bicycles were regarded at that time with even graver suspicion than cars, and it was not always easy to find a clear, safe piece of road for this. The stretch between Barnet and Hatfield, we discovered, was the best around north London, and along here at night my great friend Jack Withers and I used to test our Rexs and later our Indians at speeds and under conditions that I prefer not to think about now.

Just as it is today, the Isle of Man Tourist Trophy was the premier event in the calendar, and—greatly daring—I entered my name for it, was accepted, and in due course took the boat to Douglas with my Rex. It was a wonderful course that extended across the width of the island and included every conceivable sort of corner and gradient, and wherever I went there were famous drivers I had read about and idolized, and every variety of fast machine. I was quite mad, I thought, to be pitting myself against this phalanx of works' entries and terribly experienced professionals.

Against the name W. O. Bentley in the 1909 records there is the bald and humbling entry: 'Crashed'. Actually I didn't survive a lap, overdoing it on one of the corners where over-hanging trees had left a film of dampness on the road. Half-way round I knew I wasn't going to make it, and there is little you can do about a dry-stone wall beyond waiting to hit it when you are skidding at 50 m.p.h. Luckily that wall was low enough, or I was tall enough, for me to take the brunt of the shock with my chest instead of my head, and I was only bruised and winded.

Brooklands had been open for two years by then and there were regular motor-cycling races there. One of the most important was the One-Hour in August, and in spite of the T.T. débâcle, I decided to have a go with the Rex. Motor cycling on Brooklands was not so uncomfortable as many people might imagine, firstly because the track was in quite good condition in those days, and also because we could not go very fast—sixty was about our maximum—and therefore never strayed up on to the rougher part near the top of the bankings, In fact that vast expanse of concrete was a little intimidating after the narrow I.O.M. roads.

I don't think I should have even finished, let alone managed to secure quite a good second, in that race if I had not incorporated a modification of my own in the Rex, which fed a film of oil into the carburettor by way of a little pipe from the crank-case. This made a tremendous difference to the performance; in fact after I told the Rex people about it, I rather think they incorporated it in all their models.

One of my last efforts on the 3½ Speed Model Rex was the 6-Days Trial, a sustained and demanding event which took place mostly over the Welsh hills, the centre being Shrewsbury. Every day we went out on timed runs between controls and up some of those formidable hills. Like most trials it was regularity and not speed that counted, though the set speed up some of the mountains did take some keeping up. It was an interesting and enjoyable business, and from it I learnt a lot that was to come in useful when I transferred my loyalty to four wheels. Like the London–Edinburgh and most other trials there was no outright winner; it was a Gold Medal, a Silver one or nothing, and with 1,320 points out of a possible 1,335 I was lucky enough to qualify for the Gold.

One of my heroes at this time was Lee Evans, a superb rider in the Rex team who helped me a great deal in all my preparation and racing. Everything he said or did was right so far as I was concerned; so when he transferred to Indians, along I went too. The Indian was an American machine, and I suppose the Gilera of its day. It was a dream 'bike, with chain drive and terrific performance; but what I loved most about it was its silence. I have put up with a lot of noise in my time, but I don't like it, and I hate noise for the sake of noise. To me 70 m.p.h. in silence is far more creditable than a noisy 80 m.p.h. I am quite sure that the 1910 Indians were quieter than any air-cooled motor cycle on the market today, regardless of performance; and this feature was not only pleasant but useful at a time when the police were much hotter than they are today about noisy exhausts. In fact the rider of any modern police motor bicycle would have been in court in no time before the First World War.

With this Indian, I thought, I really ought to be able to do something, for it was astonishingly fast as well as a beautiful machine to ride. Kop Hill Climb, the first thing I tried it on, proved this, and to my astonishment and terrific satisfaction I went up in 1 min. 27 sec., even beating several of the professionals there like Wells and Lee Evans on similar machines.

T.T. time came round again and I decided to sacrifice my holiday and have another crack. And I wasn't going to do anything silly this time. I had learnt a lot since the previous event both about riding and preparation, and it was going to be a case of 'no trouble's too much'. My ambition, like that of so many independent drivers since the earliest days of motor sport, was to beat the official works' team.

Well, I was unlucky, and I don't think for once it is unfair to say that. The Indian really was in fine fettle, as it ought to have been after all the time I had expended on it, and I think it was the fastest Indian on the island. The start was individual machine by machine, as it is today and was in the early T.T. car races, and I went off towards Ballacraine riding faster than I had ever ridden in my life. I passed Godfrey without too much trouble, and even got by Jack Marshall, the champion hill-climber, and completed the lap in 19 min. 27 sec., faster than all the Indians.

I was bursting with confidence and thoroughly enjoying myself on the second lap when suddenly my rear tyre burst, sending me in a terrific skid towards a wall. Here we go again, I thought, and maybe this time I shan't be so lucky! But I managed to pull up somehow on the verge, and when I had reorientated myself, took a look at the wheel. It was a terrible mess. The tube was in ribbons and the tyre had wrapped itself round and round the rim, damaging it hopelessly. There was nothing for it but to retire, horribly disappointed and cursing the makers of the tyres I had changed to (along with all the other Indians) the day before. The works' team had just the same trouble, and what should have been an Indian walk-over turned out a disaster, with only one finishing.

However, it wasn't a completely fruitless trip, for the next day there was the hill-climb up Snaefell. This time we used the old tyres and everything went swimmingly—especially for me, as I just managed to beat Lee Evans and Franklin and put up fastest time.

There was one more race and one more machine I should say a few words about. The race was the One-Hour T.T. at Brooklands, an all-Indian benefit with Bennet leading me home by half a mile. And the machine was the 5-h.p. Indian, which ran 1–2–3 in the next Isle of Man T.T. The attractions of the motor car were already getting a firm hold on me when I bought that big Indian, and I think I was probably prejudiced against it before I even sat in the saddle. Anyway, I didn't care for it, kept it for only a short time, and when I made the exchange it was for a 9-h.p. Riley car—of which more later.

That was the end of motor cycling for me, at least for thirty-odd years. We are jumping a long way ahead if I mention the Francis Barnett here, but as I've said I would keep all my motor cycling in this chapter, perhaps I had better say that it was a splendid little 98 c.c. machine bought originally in the interests of petrol economy when I had to travel daily between the Lagonda works and my home in World War Two, and also add that it not only gave me a great deal of quiet excitement in my fifties, but also kept me entirely free from the common cold. In short, I can recommend motor cycling not only as an agreeable and exhilarating, but also an extremely healthy, means of transport.

4

CABS AND CONCESSIONS

THE London taxi-cab has never been distinguished for advanced design or liveliness, and a 1910 two-cylinder Unic was perhaps an odd training ground for someone whose life was to be spent with high-performance machines. But my two years with those worthy sloggers[1] probably taught me as much as I could have learnt anywhere.

It all began with that letter to E. M. P. Boileau. He put me in touch with a man called Greathead who was the general manager of the National Motor Cab Company. So I went along to Hammersmith one day and landed myself the job of assistant to the second-in-command, a fellow called E. C. Esse, who really ran everything in the place except the finances, which Greathead kept under his wing. I liked Esse right away, liked his quiet, soothing manner and the feeling he gave of efficiency. He was very tall, with a bristling moustache and spectacles. Later we discovered our mutual passion for photography, and that helped to cement our friendship.

There were a lot of cab companies then, competition was fierce, and although the National had two hundred and fifty bright-red cabs, it was by no means the biggest. The little fish were always being eaten up by the bigger fish, and unless we were careful, I was warned, that could easily happen to us. Cab-running was a fine-marginal business. A healthy profit could be made, but any extravagance or wastefulness could convert this to a heavy loss in no time. Everything, in fact,

---

[1] They were all landaulettes, with as generous luggage and passenger space as the modern cab, and as all-square and erect as the Americans imagine our cabs are today.

45

depended on running efficiency; and this was where I came in. I was given the nominal rank of General Assistant, but actually I was a sort of odd-body cum efficiency specialist.

On my first morning I had a little lecture from Esse, who explained that the cabs were the company's property and responsibility, that we had to maintain them, overhaul them, service them every night, engage and pay the drivers.

'What we've got to do, Bentley,' he told me, 'is to try to cut down on the cost of these overhauls—in fact all our running costs.'

He led me out of his office, introduced me to some of the mechanics, to a few of the drivers waiting to go out, and to the great hefty tough nut, Colborn, who was in charge of them.

'And you must meet Hussein,' Esse said, leading me towards this formidable-looking Frenchman. 'He's our foreman. You'll find him quite unique.'

I was to have a lot to do with Hussein and wondered how I was going to get on with him. As things turned out we got on admirably. He was a good engineer, like so many Frenchmen, a good mechanic, and he became a good friend. He had only one weakness, and this was for absinthe. For weeks on end all would be quiet at Hammersmith; then suddenly, for no apparent reason, Hussein would get hold of a bottle, and all hell was let loose. He would drink prodigious quantities of it and go completely berserk, tearing round the shops brandishing an outsize spanner and threatening to 'Keel you all!' It was most alarming. But the next day he was as quiet and courteous as ever.

At Hammersmith the grounding I had had at Doncaster in the technique of human relations proved its value. Although I had no direct authority over the drivers, I had a lot to do with them, and I found them quite tricky at first. Cab drivers the world over are an independent race and the Hammersmith men were as independent as any. It was no good playing the heavy father, taking a 'holier-than-thou' attitude, or treating obstreperousness in a jocular 'one-of-the-boys' manner. Labour relations, for want of a better term, can be learnt only by experience, and I really can't define their formula, but it includes the ability to take a ribbing the right way. Sometimes —but only as a last resort—I would hail one of our cabs in the West End late at night, and then there would be no peace the next day. 'Bentley gallivanting round the bright lights again last night—coo, 'e's a masher, Bentley is!' There was never a dull moment with the drivers. They used to put up a ring at the works sometimes and have a few bouts. The antagonism was terrific and the standard of boxing very high. I used to bring friends along for a cheap show and it was always a roaring success. 'Much better than anything you see at the Wonderland,' they used to tell me.

The National cab drivers were a good and likeable bunch; but a few of them were a bit sharp, and one or two downright dishonest. These gave us an enormous amount of trouble because it was so difficult to pin down the culprits, let alone find any proof that we were being done. I got on to the first clue some time during my first few weeks when I was up in Birmingham on some mission or other and happened to see a red Unic carrying our registration numbers. I thought it was odd, a hundred-mile fare being almost beyond the capacity of the Unic anyway, and when I returned I checked on the records and found that this cab had recorded a total of forty-five miles for the day.

I reported my suspicions to Esse, who told me that he had known that this sort of thing had been going on for some time, but that he had had nothing concrete to go on. Even now it was not simply a matter of confronting the driver and accusing him. He would probably just deny it, put on an offended air and walk out. It was just as likely that a dozen of his cronies would follow him to General or one of our other competitors; and, there being no surplus of skilled cabbies, they would be welcomed with open arms.

Esse, Colborn and I set about our detective work with

great discretion, and a silent battle of wits now ensued, with neither side acknowledging this state of cold war. Our own MI5 put us on to the next clue. The cab meters were operated through a cable from a scroll on the offside front wheel, and it took only a few minutes to change wheels in a quiet side street. They would then operate for the best part of a day with a 'faulty' meter. 'Sorry, sir, the meter's gone wrong, sir.' They probably added dramatic effect by banging the thing, muttering 'Must get it fixed,' and slipping into their pocket the agreed estimated fare for the trip, plus the tip. It was a highly profitable business, with all costs met by the firm.

We opened the attack by sealing the scroll and checking on all the seals every twenty-four hours. This was answered by pulling the tube carrying the cable down through the floorboards and taking the pin out. We then sealed the tube. The opposition got round this one too. They were an ingenious bunch who were obviously enjoying this sport from sheer deviltry as much as for the profit. We sealed the wheel nuts, sealed the cable, sealed half the nuts in desperation, until the cabs were going round with several pounds of dead-weight lead and wire on their chassis.

But they were still cheating us. It finally took months to find the answer, and I must have put in dozens of hours puzzling over it before quite by chance I discovered a minute hole in the glass over one of the meters. I saw at once that a needle could be delicately inserted through this and manipulated to hitch back the mileage figures. We knew that there were only a few specialists in London who could carry out such fine drilling work. For the next step we decided to call in professional aid.

I think our detective enjoyed the few days he spent with us. He was a cheerful fellow who quite entered into the spirit of the game. We dressed him as a driver and introduced him around the other men. The turnover of drivers being heavy, that went off all right. Then he went out on the trail. The operation, he eventually discovered, was a simple one, carried out at a little

Above : The first experimental 3-litre Bentley engine

Below : Pennel sits beside me as mechanic before the start of our first big race, the 1922 T.T.

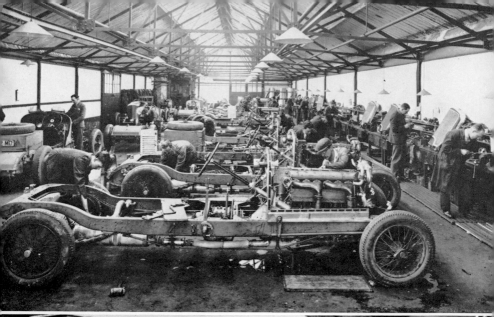

Above: A line of 6½-litre chassis, *circa* 1929

Below: The works at Oxgate Lane, Cricklewood. The Welsh Harp in the background

place near King's Cross for a modest sum. We thanked and paid our detective—and that was the end of the drain on our fare money. Our labour relations remained happy, and no word of accusation had been exchanged throughout the campaign.

That was the most exciting challenge I had at Hammersmith. Otherwise my two years with the National, whose motto might have been *ne quid nimis*, were mainly occupied with economy measures. Once a year the cabs had to be detached from their chassis and body and chassis overhauled for the police inspection and certification. This was a most expensive business, and I did battle with the coach-builder to bring down to the minimum the cost of his side of the operation. We streamlined the regular works maintenance and devised a new and rather revolutionary method of dealing with the worn dogs on the gears—by simply welding on new ones. Top gear on the Unic was a terror and sometimes nearly dislocated your wrist, which led to expensive dog wear. Fuel costs were a constant enemy, too, and the target for periodic harassing attacks. I spent hours with those carburettors, to the disapproval of the drivers who strongly resented losing any of their meagre performance. One major jet modification I installed in all the cabs aroused the strongest suspicion, and a hearty laugh and a word of reassurance were called for. 'Don't worry,' I told them, 'this'll give you just that extra power you want,' a deceit that matched even the meter-fiddling of some of the rogues among them.

At first I motor-biked to Hammersmith from Avenue Road, where I was still living with my family, but the lure of four wheels was becoming stronger and I was actually earning some money now instead of living off an allowance provided by my mother out of my future inheritance. Some of this new income went on the Riley, my first car, and, like most first cars, the one I remember best of all the many I have owned. It was a 9-h.p. V-twin-cylinder machine with the engine under the seat and with chain drive. It may not have been very

D

susceptible to tuning, in spite of all my efforts, but it was quite
lively and gave me a lot of fun. But it did have one serious
vice: partly because of its very short wheel-base, it was equally
eager to travel backwards as forwards. The slightest incline
combined with the least little bit of grease on the road set it off
in the reverse direction, and there was not much you could do
about it. After a time this became less humorous and more
tedious, so I exchanged it at the Sizaire-Naudin concessionaires
for one of their more sporty four-cylinder machines. Now I had
some real performance and a more rewarding engine on which
to work. The Sizaire-Naudin had a good record in Voiturette
racing in France, and as soon as I had mine out on the road I
began to see why. She had nice positive steering, held the road
magnificently with her independent front suspension and was
a joy at speed.

.   .   .   .   .

The year 1911 was happy and exciting. Life was opening up
for me, and I liked what I saw. I was independent, the severity
of apprenticeship behind me, with a comfortable home, a
reasonable salary (augmented by racing tips of incredible
accuracy from a driver at the works, who well deserved his
25% share of the winnings) and many good friends. There
were Henry Wood Promenade Concerts at Queen's Hall, and
of course music-halls at the Palace and Empire, with late
suppers at the Piccadilly to the music of de Groute's orchestra
to round off an evening. And there was Leonie Gore, Jack
Withers' stepsister. Jack and I had many things in common,
our strongest bond being first our Rex and Indian motor
cycles and then our cars. We often ended up at his house at
Maresfield Gardens, Hampstead, and there for the first time I
met my future wife.

I can't say the response was very enthusiastic at first, and
for some time there was a certain lack of balance between the
affection we felt for one another. She was accustomed to the

comforts of life, and I must have realized that at twenty-two I was in no position to give her what she expected. If I didn't, her parents made the fact clear to me. However, I was doggedly persistent, and prepared to wait.

Life may have been full and happy enough, and I enjoyed my job at Hammersmith, but I was not contented. For years the locomotive had monopolized my thoughts and ruled my ambitions. At the completion of my apprenticeship, and my departure from King's Cross, there had been no disillusion-ment. Like all first loves of childhood, warm with early memories and associations, the railway engine held a special place in my heart, and nothing would ever quite take its place. We remained friends after we parted and have remained on the best of terms to this day. But now the motor car, which I had once approached with caution, perhaps still with a trace of suspicion and certainly with strictly materialistic motives, had become firmly entrenched. Two hundred and fifty lines—which grew to 500 during my term—a decidedly odd Riley and a Sizaire-Naudin had been mainly responsible for this. The attraction of the power and speed of the motor car, the realiza-tion of the independence and the means to take you over a great distance that it offered, came to me at a period of growing self-confidence and coincided with a keen wish to make more money and to be my own master.

My chance came when I was ripe and eager for it, but quite unexpectedly, in the early months of 1912. My brother, L.H., had decided that farming was an unprofitable business after all—and from the way he managed it this was a natural conclusion—and was looking round for something in which invest his money. H.M., glancing through the classified advertisements one day, thought he might have found it. A firm called Lecoq and Fernie, concessionaires for several French cars, was looking for a new director, complete with money. H.M. went along to see if this would do for his brother.

It was not a very satisfactory interview, with H.M. trying

his hardest to sell L.H. to Lecoq, the sharp and amusing director who was also chairman and managing director of a firm of trunk and suitcase manufacturers, Vuitton Trunks. Lecoq, H.M. reported later, appeared to have a single-minded interest in making money, and he also got the impression that he was a good deal more interested in making it out of luggage than motor cars.

'You'd better come and see my fellow director, Fernie,' H.M. was told. 'He knows much more about it than I do.'

Major Fernie was a different sort of proposition altogether, in appearance resembling a caricature in *Punch* of the rough-riding cavalry officer (which actually I think he had been), complete with aggressive ginger moustache; a big, domineering man who fancied himself as the straight-from-the-shoulder business man who does not mince his words.

H.M. stood up to the verbal barrage well enough, but found himself forced to agree that a half-hearted foray into farming did not necessarily equip you for an active director-ship in a motor-car concession. The interview took an unex-pected turn.

'Now what about you? Qualified chartered accountant—just the man we're looking for. Got any money?'

Embarrassed, H.M. stalled. 'Well, er—I'll think it over. It's rather difficult, you see . . .'

The outcome of all this led to a delicate family situation.

'But this is just the kind of opening Walter's been looking for.'

'And he's had the right kind of training for it.'

'What do they want an accountant for?'

H.M. agreed warmly with them all, and said he would not dream of depriving me of the chance. I said the same thing as emphatically in different words. Impasse.

Then H.M. grinned at me and said, 'Let's toss for it.'

At the time my whole future seemed to depend on that spinning coin, but as it turned out it was not very important that I won. Either way, I think, Lecoq and Fernie would have become Bentley and Bentley within a few months.

My share in the business cost me £2,000, which again came out of the money I would inherit when my mother died. I handed in my notice at the National Motor Cab Company, said good-bye to Greathead, Esse, Colborn, the gay quixotic Hussein, the motley army of drivers, the whole noisy, buzzing hive of hundreds of sturdy Unics. I was to miss certain things at the National, but I was content never again to peer under one of those identical red bonnets at one of those identical two-cylinder engines. After two years with them, to deal with another machine was a refreshingly exciting thought.

Lecoq and Fernie had the concession for three makes of French cars: Buchet, La Licorne and Doriet, Flandrin et Parent. But two were disposed of just before I arrived, and I was thankful it was the D.F.P. that had been retained. This French car interested me a great deal, and I thought it had real possibilities.

The first thing I did at the Hanover Street office was to sit down and wonder why any D.F.P.s at all had been sold; with the sort of promotion they had been receiving, with no road tests and no advertising, it was a miracle that they had kept up the rate to one a month. It said something for the word-of-mouth reputation of the car, I suppose, but I did see why they had inserted that invitation in the classified columns.

I began by trying to work up some sort of enthusiasm in Hanover Street, and it took only a week or two to discover that there wasn't any. Lecoq was too busy turning over profitable suitcases and trunks, and his partner appeared to have given up in despair long ago. The mask of the hard-driving business man fell away, revealing a noisy, bossy, ineffectual man—who tried to push me around. Now I hate being pushed as violently as I hate pushing others; it doesn't work with me, and I know it would never have brought results (or made for pleasant working conditions) if I had ever tried it on anyone working with me. I have never ordered anyone to do anything in all my life.

I made it amply clear to Lecoq that I was not going to be pushed around, and one way and another we exchanged quite a few words.

It would have been all too easy to slip into the general air of disillusion in that office, and come to the conclusion that I had given up my job and thrown myself—and my money—into a dead concern. But I knew how profitable a good foreign-car concession could be; there were Charles Jarrott and Letts, Warwick Wright and many others to bear witness to this. And I knew business in the motor trade was good, and that the D.F.P. had virtually no competition on the British market. I was completely confident that this sporty little well-made French car could be sold in good numbers if it was only given a chance.

I talked things over with H.M. 'The company will never get anywhere with this man Fernie, and Lecoq's nothing but a sleeping partner,' I told him. 'A child of five knows more about selling motor cars than they do.'

Neither of us could understand why they had ever obtained the concession in the first place, and having obtained it, why they did not do something about it, or sell out.

'Do you think they would?' H.M. suddenly asked.

I said I thought it was worth investigating, and he already knew my opinion that there were tremendous possibilities in the D.F.P., and agreed with me.

'Let's go and ask them then,' H.M. said; and that is what we did.

I think Lecoq and Fernie were delighted when we opened negotiations for the purchase by H.M. of their share in the business. Thinking about it now, I am sure that this is just what they had hoped would happen, and certainly their attempt to appear as reluctant vendors was not very convincing. Oh, but how those two could haggle! The negotiations were interminable, and before we had finished a couple of Lecoq's suitcases became involved in the bidding. In the end we took the suitcases and they took £2,000 from H.M. for their shares.

.   .   .   .   .   .

This was the most daring and momentous thing either H.M. or I had ever done. When all the document-signing and hand-shaking were over, we eyed one another nervously. We were twenty-four and twenty-seven, and had a £4,000 business (which was regarded—when it was regarded at all—as moribund) on our hands.

But we went home in a state of tremendous excitement and bursting with enthusiasm. Our chance had come, and we were going to build up this company, put the name of D.F.P. on the map and make a lot of money. There was nothing to hold us back now.

The new company of Bentley and Bentley moved in in March, 1912, with far too little working capital and far too much confidence. The showrooms we kept in Hanover Street; H.M., who was to look after the sales and business side, worked there with his secretary, while I moved into an old coach-house we rented from J. H. Easter, who did the body trimming for us, in New Street Mews off Upper Baker Street.[1] To work at Hanover Street as manager we had G. P. de Freville, an excellent man, whose inherent pessimism was no bad thing, for the bubbles of optimism in those early days needed puncturing from time to time. De Freville was a realist, and a worker. He had to be to survive the pressure, for we all worked at a tremendous pace for long hours week after week until we achieved our ambition and began to show a profit after the first six months. After the war, de Freville was to help launch the Alvis Car Company.

---

[1] Seven years later, in this same coach-house, the first 3-litre Bentley engine Ex I roared into life, to the alarm of the local inhabitants. Today there is a plaque on the wall commemorating the occasion.

After a short time we got over from the French factory a little wizard called Leroux as head—and only—mechanic. Leroux was another tremendous worker whom we soon came to regard as the very backbone of Bentley and Bentley. He achieved prodigies of labour in the two and a half years he worked for us, acting as liaison with the factory, tuning and preparing the cars for competition work and riding as mechanic in races—an onerous and dangerous duty outside his routine work of checking over the chassis when they arrived from France, and servicing owners' cars.

Our first figures above the red line were not very imposing, but they did spur us on. There was no doubt that we were on the right track: selling the right product at the right price, and with some show of energy and initiative. We had three models in the catalogue, the 10–12 h.p., the 12–15 and the 16–20, at prices from £265 to £550, with a wide choice of bodywork, built by Harrison of Stanhope Street. The 10–12 was a pleasant enough little motor car, a sporty two-seater with a well-raked windscreen and a fair turn of speed. We never pushed the 16–20, a heavy, sluggish car with little more character than dozens of British-made competitors. But the 12–15 was a different proposition.

There was nothing available elsewhere quite like the 12–15 D.F.P., and it was on this model that I had based my confidence in our future. In France it was considered a reliable, steady family four-seater; but then the French have always had different standards of performance from the English, and there were no cars of the same capacity on English roads then that could keep up with it. It was much livelier than the 12-h.p. Humber, but what made it even more interesting to me was the susceptibility of the 70 × 130 mm. four-cylinder engine to tuning. There was real potential here, and since H.M. and I had decided from the beginning that the quickest and most effective publicity came from racing and other competition work, it was on one of these engines that I set Leroux to work in May, easing things up generally and increasing the compression. I had my eye on the Aston hill-climb in June. I thought we had a chance of putting up a fair show.

. . . . .

It turned out a brilliantly fine Saturday morning, and the sun was already hot when Leonie and I set off for Tring in the open two-seater D.F.P. De Freville was there to see us away, full of encouragement of course, as usual. 'You'll get some nice dust up in the Chilterns today,' he told us with a shake of his head.

But he wished us luck, too, and this we were going to need. It was the first time I had ever tackled competition work on four wheels and I was feeling thoroughly nervous about the prospect of competing against experienced hill-climb drivers in one of the most important events of the season. I could face making a fool of myself in front of Leonie better than I could the prospect of failure with a machine we were working desperately to put on the map. There was an awful lot at stake, I realized, as we drove out through Hendon and Watford, and I thanked heaven that at least the weather was cheerful (to blazes with de Freville and his dust!) and the car was running beautifully.

A pleasant drive in a nice open car with your fiancée beside you cheers up most people, however, and I felt more hopeful about things when we got to Aston. But my optimism fell with a thump again after I had had a chance of looking round the other drivers and cars. In the gay party atmosphere everyone seemed to be on familiar terms with everyone else, they all seemed to 'belong' in the most natural way, and to be self-assured to a degree that at once depressed and exasperated me. I was glad H.M. was there (he had come up in another car on his own), and glad to have Leonie to ease the sense of isolation.

Most of the cars, I noticed, were foreign: Stoewers, De

Dions, Oryxs, Chenard-Walckers, Le Guis and Pilots, together
with several English Humbers and Scottish Arrol-Johnstons. In
my class, the 2-litre Class 2, the virtually unassailable champion
was W. G. Tuck, who always drove a Humber and was tester
for that firm. Against him—and against a good deal of other
potent machinery—I could see that my chances were not taken
very seriously, and the defeatism I could feel rising up as I took
my place in the queue leading to the start had to be firmly
suppressed.

One after another we watched the 2-litre cars go away
amid blasting exhaust roar and a scream of high revs that
echoed against the high bank and rolled away through the
beeches; and with each departure we moved closer to the
starting line. It was an afternoon for record breaking, and Tuck
and one of the Vinot drivers had already done very fast runs
when I gently eased the D.F.P. on to the white line and drew
on the hand-brake. Later I learnt every inch of the Aston climb,
but at that moment I hadn't the least idea of the way the
corners went beyond the general course described by the
succession of dust trails that had preceded me up the hill. I
pulled down my goggles and hoped for the best.

Success or failure in hill-climbing is measured in tenths of
seconds, which are usually gained or lost at certain points on
the course. Because of the very steep initial gradient at Aston,
it was the change from first to second a few yards from the line
that counted. I had made a point of practising this frequently,
and I snicked the lever back without touching the clutch and
at revs for which the D.F.P. was never intended. Once away,
my nerve-storm and self-consciousness seemed to disappear,
and as the track levelled off and I changed to third, I could see
the first left-hander ahead. It was third gear all the time then,
with the right foot hard on the boards: up the rising gradient,
through the sharp right-hander, and on and up to the finish at
the top.

Leonie seemed to have enjoyed every wild second of the
ride. When I pulled up she smiled through a mask of grey dust

and congratulated me. In her innocence she even thought we must have broken the record.

As a certain contradiction to her claim, the loudspeaker announcement came over a few moments later: 'Here is the time for Mr. W. O. Bentley's D.F.P. . . .' There was a horrible pause which I filled by trying to remember whether the time he had given was good or bad. Then: 'This is the fastest time of the day for Class 2 and is a record for a 2-litre car at Aston. It also makes the D.F.P. the day's winner on Formula.' So Leonie had been right after all!

We were wildly excited, and as we were congratulated from all sides, that acute sense of alienation, of being an interloper in a hostile world, subsided. I was going to enjoy giving the news to de Freville.

Aston marked among other things for me my first brush with Tuck in a ding-dong battle on a number of fields during the next two and a half years. As we drove away I sensed that he was already thirsting for revenge.

.   .   .   .   .

The success at Aston was a start, but it takes more than a class win at a hill-climb to establish a reputation. However, we took full advantage of this little effort by putting the car, with an accompanying notice, in the showrooms, booking some modest advertising space, and generally spreading the word about that, for those who liked it, there was real performance in the D.F.P. What was most important, it gave encouragement to our distributors and agents and supported my campaign which was opening new markets in the provinces.

D.F.P. had never had area distributors in the past, and one of the first things I had done was to go on a tour round the country trying to find them. It required a lot of persuasion and was the most exhausting work I had ever encountered. While the motor trade was nothing like the tightly knit, virtually impregnable organization that it is today, by 1912 it had already formed a hard skin that was difficult to penetrate, and since March most of my life seemed to have been spent in dim, smoky hotel bars from Newcastle to Bristol, talking, talking, talking D.F.P. to dealers. I had not managed too badly with most of them, and already the results could be seen in the steadily growing stream of orders from those agents whom I had first persuaded to take appointments. Only in the Midlands did I strike real trouble. For some reason the fact that I had not 'come up through bicycles' seemed to stick in a few of the Midlanders' throats. I suppose fundamentally it was the old class barrier raising its ugly head, even if it was in inverted form. Heaven knows, I don't want to generalize about the Midlander, let alone condemn him, for I have a number of good friends in that part of the country. But this seems a good a point at which to confess that I have never found business relations easy with some of the high-powered, straight-talking, as-good-as-the-next-man tycoons of the Midland car distributing trade. It is a thing I regret because, apart from anything else, both sides have suffered as a result.

It would be charitable to think that some interest in the D.F.P. by the motoring press was spontaneously aroused by our early competition successes, but it did happen that this coincided with our taking some advertising space. A decent interval passed after our first bookings, and then followed requests for test cars, and, shortly after, the reports were published.

We could not have asked for better—'an excellent turn of speed', 'splendid power and flexibility', a 'sweet clutch', 'smooth brakes'; and it had shown a 'meritorious performance' in competition. H.M. and I decided to take some more advertising, which we could not afford, but if these were the results, it was foolish to continue to rely solely on word-of-mouth goodwill. We also had to have a stand at the Motor Show at Olympia, though this would stretch our resources to breaking point. For this, membership of the Society of Motor Manufacturers and Traders was necessary, so we duly joined.

What we needed, I realized, was something to back up our

first appearance at the Show, something beyond a success or two at hill-climbs. The idea of a special-bodied record-breaking D.F.P. had been forming in my mind for some time, and one day I put it to H.M.

'I've got my eyes on those Class B records,' I told him. 'We're getting nearly 70 m.p.h. out of the tuned 12–15. If we got Harrisons to work on a single-seat aluminium body, I think we might stand a chance.'

'It would be a good thing if we could pip Tuck again,' he agreed. 'But it'll take some doing.'

The Humber held all the records in this class, and I confess that spurred us on. Harrisons did a quick, neat job, and the humble 12–15 looked quite formidable in its new narrow polished aluminium suit, with streamlined tail astern and disc wheels. As before, we did no other modifications beyond increasing the compression and cleaning and loosening up with great care all round.

H.M., Leroux and I went down to Brooklands on November 9th, just after Tuck's records had been pipped by Reid's Arrol-Johnston, and with no spectators beyond Colonel Lindsay Lloyd, the timekeeper, I did a few warming-up laps and then cracked off.

You could call that first attempt a qualified success. Certainly we did not do all we had hoped for, but we gained a lot of useful experience, and we did manage to raise the ten-laps record from just over 60 m.p.h. to 66.78. We should have to be content with that for our Motor Show publicity.

· · · · ·

An endurance trial that never got into any record book was a run of 635 miles that H.M. and I made on a sad mission. My brother Arthur—A.W.—a wonderful personality who seemed always to be overflowing with vivacity and enterprise and high spirits, died suddenly of a throat infection that modern drugs could have cured in a day or two. It was a great blow to the family, and especially to H.M., who was nearest to him in age and had the greatest affection for him. With his enormous sense of fun and humour, A.W. had a romantic streak, and he had expressed a wish that his ashes should be scattered in a valley near Achanalt in Ross and Cromarty where he had often spent happy fishing holidays.

I thought it would take H.M.'s mind off the funeral if we made this the occasion for an endurance run, and I knew the idea of a non-stop drive—and at that time 600 miles was a very long drive—would have appealed to Arthur. So we set off in a two-seater 12–15 D.F.P. at 2.45 one dark wet December afternoon, H.M. driving through the rain, without wipers of course, as far as Grantham, which we reached at 6.40. We refuelled, had a quick drink at the George, and I drove on to Doncaster. By this time our acetyline cylinder was getting low and the headlights were noticeably dimming, so we spent a fruitless half hour hunting up a new one.

Still in teeming rain and in pitch darkness, we reached Newcastle at two in the morning, driving on sidelights, gave up the hunt round the garages after an hour or so, and drove on again with an electric torch strapped to a front wing. We had a ten-minute stop at Berwick, then I drove straight through to Edinburgh, stopping there for breakfast—our only sit-down meal—and the acetyline.

There was snow on the Stirling hills when we left at noon, and soon we were deep in it up in the Grampians. But at least the weather cleared, and we had a moon to help us along the narrow, winding tracks that were marked as roads on the map. Inverness was reached at a quarter to eight in the evening, and there we stopped only for petrol and carried straight on past Beauly Firth, Loch Garve and Loch Luichart, arriving at Achanalt thirty-one hours after our start from London, dead tired and stiff and cramped, but feeling, I think, that we had done the right thing.

.   .   .   .   .

We struggled through the lean motoring months of 1912–13 and found we could face the new season with reasonable confidence. The little niche we had cut out for ourselves demanded a full competition programme, and we started off well by cleaning up at Aston as positively as the year before. At Shelsley Walsh, where the cars were not divided into classes, we clocked 1 min. 27 sec., which was better than some of the bigger cars and was not beaten by anything with a smaller engine.

At Brooklands I entered for the first time in a race, the Whitsun Handicap meeting, and came up against Tuck again. He just beat me into second place, and then followed this up by beating all the Class B records from the half mile to ten laps at speeds up to nearly 82 m.p.h. This made us think a bit; and led us to the conclusion that something more drastic than hitherto would have to be done to the engine.

I decided I should have to go over to France to have words with M. Doriot, less to ask for advice than to discover whether he could incorporate any successful modifications we might make as standard on the 12–15s for English export. What we had in mind, besides raised compression, were improvements to the induction pipe and carburetion.

Our relations with the factory had been wonderful from the start; there was always the closest co-operation and they could never do enough for us. M. Doriot, a trifle bewildered at the performance we had squeezed from his homely little vehicles, had already visited us, and when I sat in his office at Courbevoie on the outskirts of Paris late in June, 1913, he jumped at my plan to produce for us a modified 12–15 for our sportier customers. I was certain, I told him, there would be a good demand for it.

While we were talking all this over, I noticed on Doriot's desk a little decorative piston, made of some alloy, which had obviously been given to D.F.P. as a souvenir paper-weight by the firm that did their foundry work. Doriot saw me pick it up before I left. 'Pretty, isn't it?' he said. 'Aluminium, you know.'

I agreed and said nothing. But on the way back to Paris my mind played on that paper-weight. In our record-breaking attempts we had got up to around 80 m.p.h., and there we had stuck, unable to squeeze any more power out of the engine. Piston failure had marked our stalling point; very light steel pistons broke their rings, cast-iron pistons cracked. That aluminium memento succeeded in keeping me awake all the way home, and I swept into Hanover Street like an over-excited schoolboy.

H.M. heard me out, eyeing me curiously, and proceeded to recommend caution. 'But I'm sure it's the answer,' I told him. 'And there's no harm in trying. I'm going back to investigate. I'd like to have a set cast to try out in the 12–15.'

At twenty-five it takes a lot to kill enthusiasm, and even Doriot's cold douche had no effect. 'They'll break and seize up before you're doing 2,000 r.p.m.,' he said. 'Aluminium's not suitable for the strains and stresses of that sort of work.'

'Well, I think you're wrong,' I told him. 'Anyway, just let me make a call at your foundry. All we can lose is the cost of a few pistons.'

The Corbin foundry showed more interest, worked out a formula of 12% copper to 88% aluminium, and agreed to cast some for experimental work.

The pistons were with us in a few weeks, and Leroux and I got to work. We ran them with plenty of clearance and found at once that we were getting more power, so we lightened them and ran them again—and got another improvement. Then we took a chance and lightened them again, increased the compression further; still we had no trouble. After more very thorough testing, we sent the good news to France and told them that we were ready to go ahead with the modified 12–15 —to be called the Speed Model—and to back its introduction on the track.

The 12–40 Speed Model was to be outwardly distinguishable from the 12–15 by its wire wheels; mechanically the compression was to be higher, and of course the aluminium pistons were to be fitted as standard, though we were not going to advertise that. We thus became the first firm to use successfully and as standard equipment aluminium pistons, the performance from which puzzled many of our competitors and gave us a tremendous advantage.

In almost every respect they were a great advance, their only drawback being the noise they made when cold, the aluminium having a greater expansion coefficient and causing piston slap. We never had to alter the formula by even a half per cent, and it remained as the standard right through the war and well into the 'twenties in both aero and car engines. I never understood why our secret never leaked out. By the summer of 1914 there were quite a number of 12–40 D.F.P.s on the road. But the only hint was contained in an article in *The Autocar*, which suggested that some French foundry was thinking of making aluminium pistons and gave incorrect figures for the proposed formula.

Until that summer H.M. had rightly recommended extreme financial discretion, and we had been very careful, ploughing back nearly all our profits and keeping overheads to a minimum. But the 12–40 called for some modest expansion, and we got an assistant for Hanover Street and I got in a mechanic to work with Leroux, an old friend from the National Motor Cab Company called Jackson, who remained with us right through the Bentley Motors days. In addition, Doriot's young son came over to help us.

We tried out the 12–40 in the special body at Brooklands at the August B.A.R.C. meeting. Against some quite formidable opposition, we ran away with the Short Handicap race at 70.5 m.p.h., lapping once at 75.12, and a month later had another serious crack at Tuck's Class B records. This time we managed 82.38 for the half mile, 81.6 for the mile, and improved on the Humber's figures for the ten laps by over two miles an hour. This was very satisfactory, and I was just thinking that we would really have something to shout about at Olympia, where the 12–40 would be shown for the first time,

E

and that we had settled with Mr. Tuck for a while, when the blighter reappeared on the scene with his tiny gold single-seater, and knocked all our records for six, taking the ten laps up to 79.63 and half mile to 83.53 m.p.h.

This was exasperating, and I was now determined to finish off the Humber once and for all. We put in some long hours at New Street Mews, fitting two plugs to each cylinder, a Bosch dual magneto, and increasing the compression still further. Then we got busy with the drill and lightened the chassis all round. Finally we worked on the transmission, fitting the 10–12's lighter rear axle, which bent frighteningly, and using an open shaft instead of a torque tube. As a safety precaution I also did without a differential. Lambert had recently killed himself at Brooklands when his tyre burst, and sent him into a skid and turned him over. It was very likely that if the Talbot had not had a differential he would have probably been all right.

Successful record-breaking on very light machines in those days was often dependent on the wind. At Brooklands conditions were ideal when it was blowing strongly from the north-east; so that you got plenty of support from behind along the straight. It was often a tedious business waiting for a wind that might give you an extra two or three miles an hour, and I just did not have the time to spare to hang around the club-house.

On 14th February I took the single-seater out with Leroux, H.M. and young Doriot—and the wind, good and strong, was of course from the south-west.

'What's to stop us going round the wrong way?' I asked.

I had certainly never thought of this before; nor, it seemed, had the officials. The rules were consulted, but there did not appear to be anything to forbid lapping clockwise, and it was certainly the obvious thing to do on a timed run.

I did one or two trial laps and the ride was no more, though certainly no less, uncomfortable than on the more orthodox anti-clockwise circuit. 'I think this is going to be all right,' I told

H.M. when I drew in. 'I don't think there'll be any trouble except coming down the banking to the fork. That's very rough.'

I survived the bumps and that nasty turn, and the single-seater behaved faultlessly, to give us everything from the half mile at 89.7 to the ten laps; all of them better than the Class C records, too.

Tuck retired from the combat after that. This settled our record-breaking tussles, but the competition continued as keenly as ever on other fields. At the speed trials at Porthcawl, for instance, I beat him home in the class event, but in the open he got far enough ahead to spray me with wet sand—that sort of thing could happen at speed trials in those days—and just pipped me. Class 2 at Aston had become a D.F.P. benefit, and my fastest time was backed up by Jack Withers' Formula win in another 12–40. Tuck would probably have beaten me at Caerphilly, but he misjudged one of the corners and as a consequence lost fastest time by 2 1/5th sec., with Jack Withers running third in his 12–40. Neither of us took the honours at the Leicestershire Hill Climb; they went to Fedden on the Straker-Squire after I lost my gear lever on that first violent change into second.

On one of our record attempts—I forget exactly which it was, but we were after the One-Hour—Dick Lisle was running simultaneously in his 3,817 c.c. Star for the Class E records. So that we should not get tangled up, I was sent away after Lisle had done half a lap, the timekeepers reckoning that at 81 m.p.h. he would gain fifty yards a lap and so would not have to pass the D.F.P. But instead, our little 2-litre machine began averaging around 83 m.p.h., and to Lisle's discomfiture I passed him quite soon.

We were all beginning to realize by then what a tremendous publicity-winning factor there was in running a small car against bigger and more powerful machines. If you won, of course, as we did sometimes, then that was wonderful, and you shouted it from the roof-tops. 'David slays Goliath' was the

headline theme then. But even if you did not, so long as you
stayed the course, the innate British sympathy for the 'little
man' who bravely battles against odds ensured the publicity.
It was what I believe the Americans call 'psychology salesmanship'; Bentley and Bentley didn't have a name for it, but we
knew we were on to a good thing.

It was this policy that decided us to enter for the fifth
International Tourist Trophy race in the Isle of Man, which,
after a lapse of five years, was due to take place on the 10th
and 11th of June. It would be certain to get more publicity
than any other race of the year, and in a car little over
half as big as all the others I reckoned we should get the
lion's share of it if we lasted out the 600 miles of rough roads
and mountain climbing. It would be an expensive business, but
worth it.

Half the motor trade and all the drivers and managers and
designers one saw around the tracks congregated in the Isle of
Man that June. I knew a lot of them by then, and many of
them—Witchell, Frank Clement, Bianchi and Tony Vandervell
—were my good friends. Tuck was there, too, of course, with
the Humber team; and so were Louis Coatalen and Laurence
Pomeroy with their Sunbeams and Vauxhalls.

It had been reported that as Boillot's Peugeot had flashed
past the post in the last *Coupe de L'Auto*, Pomeroy had turned to
Coatalen and, with a resigned shrug, had said, 'I fancy I can
see some of us going back to the office, looking up certain old
drawings, and pulling some old engines off the shelf.' Some of
the results, it appeared, were here in Douglas. Coatalen was in
his usual boisterous high spirits; Pomeroy was far less happy.
He had had a lot of trouble with his Vauxhalls, and still had
not settled satisfactorily the problem of his bolt-secured balance-
weights. Test-bed running had shown them satisfactory up to
any speed, but the violent strains and stresses caused by rapid
acceleration and deceleration in practice unfortunately told a
different story.

Besides these two makes, there was a beautifully turned-out

team of Belgian Minervas, led by their champion, Porporato, some fast Straker-Squires, and, among the less potent machinery, the Adlers and Stars and a single Hudson, suitably (or unsuitably, for it was a non-starter) modified by Rawlinson.

One or other of the Guinness brothers' Sunbeams was tipped as the likeliest winner. In spite of someone's charitable suggestion that D.F.P. stood for 'Deserves First Place', I had no illusions about our prospects. We were there for a very definite purpose, to stay the course, and unless nearly everybody else cracked up we did not stand a chance of a place.

The Isle of Man circuit was the one used by the motor bicycles today, with some severe gradients, hundreds of corners in its 37½ miles, and one climb of 1,300-odd feet up the slopes of Snaefell; but its condition in 1914 was very different. Most of the roads were of loose stones, which turned to sticky mud in rain, and as it seemed to rain almost without cessation on that island, early morning practice was mostly uncomfortable. Leroux, Doriot junior—as mechanics—H.M. and I made up the team, and we had brought two cars with us on which we had lavished hours of preparation, one for practice and the other for me to drive in the race. Regulations demanded a wider track than was standard on the 12–40, so 16–22 axles were substituted, which added two hundredweight and made us substantially heavier than any of the other cars.

The rain stopped before the start, but it had been coming down heavily all night, and this, besides making the going sticky, caused the dust-laying sodium-chloride to penetrate behind our goggles and give agonizing pain to our eyes. But we lapped at around 47 m.p.h. without too much trouble, while the two Guinness Sunbeams, which had gone straight into the lead, went round about eight miles an hour faster. The first of the Vauxhalls was out within a few minutes, its balance-weights making a rapid penetration of the crank-case; and

another followed it into retirement a lap or two later. Tuck
was out by the third lap.

Later the sun came out, making things more cheerful, and
we continued to circulate at a slightly higher speed and without a hint of trouble for the first 300 miles.

The second day was sunny and hot, so we changed tyres
from steel-studded to non-skids before refuelling and set off,
with the Guinness Sunbeams, the Minervas, Witchell's Straker-
Squire and a couple of Minervas ahead of us, Clement's
Straker-Squire, an Adler, Bianchi's Crossley and the surviving
Vauxhall following behind. Apart from the weather, everything was much the same as on the previous day, with the
sleeve-valve Minervas laying great smoke-screens from one
side of the island to the other to add to the dust menace. At one
point Leroux burnt his hand rather badly on the exhaust, but
he did not say a word at the time and I did not find out till
later. He really was the perfect mechanic to have on a long
grind like this. Even when I overdid it on a corner—the heat
and interminable noise must have made me momentarily
careless—and went for a long broadside, he just raised a wry
eyebrow and asked me solicitously if I was '*Un peu fatigué?*'

There were only six out of the twenty-three starters left at
the end, with Bill Lee Guinness romping home with a ten-
minute lead over the third Minerva. There was neither prize
nor cup for the D.F.P., though at the presentation ceremony
on the Thursday evening we did get a special medal. But
things worked out just as we had hoped they would. For all
the column-inches of free publicity and photographs we got in
the popular newspapers as well as the motoring Press, we might
almost have been first instead of last past the flag. Jack had
taken on all the giants, and if he had not killed them all he
had survived the holocaust. Variations on this theme made
good stories, we realized, as we thumbed through the stack of
Press clippings back in Hanover Street, and they all meant
increased business for us. However, stories in the newspapers—
even fairy stories—don't automatically sell motor cars; being

stern realists, we set to work to squeeze every ounce of advantage out of our success.

.   .   .   .

One of the difficulties of writing an autobiography is to keep your own life in perspective with the great events. What are my affairs and ambitions compared with the earth-shaking achievements and catastrophes of the last half century? And of what importance is the fact that two World Wars and the international slump that separated them three times turned sour for me the sweet taste of success? Particularly because I was in no real physical danger in either war, nor in severe financial trouble in the crisis, I feel it is almost inept to record that World War One killed the D.F.P., World War Two the V12 Lagonda, and that the repercussions of the Wall Street crash destroyed Bentley Motors.

The ironical thing about our effort in the T T, was that the benefit from it lasted a bare eight weeks, and we never gathered our rich harvest. We issued a new catalogue, and even got our 'Tourist Trophy Model' on the market, in that short time; but that was as far as we could go before the curtain came down.

Leonie and I had married on New Year's Day and we had had a short honeymoon touring in the West Country, but we did not find time for a real holiday until the beginning of August, when the clouds were already rolling up and the storm seemed likely to break at any minute. On the 3rd we drove down to my 'in-laws' yacht at Southampton for the Cowes Regatta. There we saw work being rushed on some destroyers at Thorneycrofts, and the atmosphere of drama and threatening disaster as Britain's ultimatum expired had already killed stone-cold the gaiety of the occasion. I decided to leave my wife on the yacht and set off back to London with my brother-in-law, Irwin Gore. We had lunch at the Bear in Farnham, and there, after the manager had politely refused to accept a five-pound note, we learnt we were at war.

The next day H.M. joined up as a Tommy. Half the Company was already gone, and there was an air of unreality in Hanover Street, and suddenly cars and motoring seemed as wildly inappropriate as yachts and regattas.

Ten days later our gallant Leroux was dead in Flanders.

5

ROTARIES

TO SIT tight and wait seemed to me the wisest thing to do for the present. Two of my brothers had joined up and had been swept away on the first great wave of volunteers, but within days the Army was suffering from indigestion; thousands of trained men, whose skill was to be desperately missed later in specialist branches of the war machine, were being wasted in infantry regiments, and thousands more were being turned away at the recruiting offices. I did try to get into one of the armoured car brigades being formed, after contacting Rolls-Royce, who had switched at once to war work and had even requisitioned for conversion Silver Ghost chassis on order for these new weapons of war. They were in touch with the Army department responsible and told me where to go, but everyone was too busy coping with the rush and suggested I should come back in a few months when things had settled down.

Trading in new cars had more or less ceased, and there was only occasional servicing work at D.F.P. to keep us occupied. The one solid contribution I did have to offer, of course, was the aluminium piston, which I thought might be of value in aero engines and was still quite unknown to any other firm in England. To pass on the specification seemed a simple enough operation until I began to think about it. Security ruled out the spreading of it broadcast among the engine manufacturers, and I realized that I should have to tread carefully. Some weeks passed before I discovered the right person to call on. He was Commander Wilfrid Briggs, and he lived in one of the little temporary wooden huts put up on the top of Admiralty Arch.

Briggs' job was to build up an engine department for the

rapidly expanding R.N.A.S., acting as liaison between the manufacturers and the Board of Admiralty. The advice I had been given was correct; he was the right man to talk to about aluminium pistons. The only officer in the Navy who could have been as clever as Briggs was the man who appointed him to this appallingly difficult post in which he had to deal with jealous, prickly engine-design departments that always knew best and often considered working for a service authority either as a favour or as beneath their dignity. He tackled bodies and individuals with an incredible tact that at once kept people happy and produced the results.

Briggs was to be my senior officer, adviser, nursemaid, champion and advocate, pacifier and moderator, for three and a half years. It wasn't until some time after my interview with him that I realized that he had me summed up and docketed within a few minutes, and from the moment I began working for him he handled me with a skill and subtlety which, allowing for the restrictions under which he worked, always got the best out of me. I owe him a great deal and am grateful to him for everything he did.

Briggs examined the piston I had brought with me and listened in silence while I did my sales talk. 'And what have you got to back up your claim?' he asked. 'It seems a remarkable thing that none of the big guns in the business have cottoned on to it after all this time.'

'It seems an odd thing to me too,' I agreed. 'I can't understand it. And I can't understand why it hasn't been developed in France. So far as I've discovered only D.F.P. know about it, and they only used it in the model they built specially for our market.'

He had heard of the D.F.P. and of some of the things we had done with it, but did not realize that we held all the Brooklands Class Records and had been virtually unbeaten in hill-climbs for a couple of years; least of all did he realize that the secret behind the power we had got out of the little engine was a new type of piston.

We talked technicalities together for a while, and then he
said: 'We've got to spread the word around about this. It's
obviously a development that's going to affect the work in all
the big design departments. We'll have to tell them about it—
but it must be done with discretion.'

Discretion meant that I had to do the job myself, he
explained, and that I must have the authority of a King's
Commission behind me.

'What on earth do you mean?' I asked.

'We must get you into uniform, Bentley,' Briggs said
blandly; and a day or two later he telephoned: 'You're an
officer now. Go to Gieves and get a uniform with two rings on
it.'

Somewhat bewildered, I went along to South Molton Street
and did as I had been told, that excellent firm providing me
with everything I needed off the peg. I stared at myself in the
full-length glass, feeling a sense of unreality which became
nightmarish when I walked out, clutching a new pair of gloves,
and received a smart salute from across the street. The reception
from my wife on the doorstep was rather less impressive! 'What
on earth's this?' she demanded.

The next day I was packed off to Derby where Rolls-Royce
were making air-cooled Renault aero engines under licence,
and working on a new design of their own. E. W. (later Lord)
Hives was in charge of the experimental department, and, with
a piston in my case, I called on him in his new office built on a
sort of island surrounded by the factory's test track.

I hadn't met him before and liked him at once. In later
years, and under sometimes trying circumstances, we were to
see a lot of one another, but we always got on well together.
He examined my piston, listened to my story, and then called
in his foundry specialist, Buchanan, to whom I gave the
formula. Very sensibly, he made an analysis to check my
figures, and then had some experimental castings made.
Production went ahead with crisis urgency, and the result was
that Rolls-Royce's first aero engine, the excellent water-cooled

200-h.p. Eagle, had aluminium instead of cast-iron or steel pistons.

From Derby I went to Sunbeams at Wolverhampton where, because I knew the squat, jovial little Louis Coatalen well, the talk was on a more informal level. 'Bentley,' he said with a puckish grin, when I had finished, 'Bentley, you're one of the best salesmen I've ever met. I wouldn't have believed it could work, but I'll take your word for it.'

Louis did; and it was used in all the Sunbeam aero engines too.

.   .   .   .   .

The next sailing orders, for the rawest, most untrained commissioned officer in the service, took me up river to Chiswick, to the Gwynne factory, not far from my old National Motor Cab works.

Gwynnes were later known for that nice little car, the 'Eight', but at that time—as they do today—they specialized in marine and water pumps. They had, however, been astute and far-sighted enough to obtain the concession for the French Clerget aero engine just before the war and were then engaged in turning these out in large numbers for Sopwiths and Nieuports. Here I was to act as another link in the chain between the manufacturer and the Admiralty, for whom they were working under contract, and put in hand experimental work that would lead to the substitution of aluminium for iron pistons in the Clerget. 'They're to do what you tell 'em to do,' Briggs had told me, a simple enough brief which I received unsuspectingly.

Neville Gwynne, the good-looking chairman, appeared to welcome me. I gathered he was a man who had to be treated circumspectly, and I was a shade uncertain whether I should be able to command the tact and patience that would be called for. I was to deal more closely with Armitage, the works manager, and he was an easier proposition; I never had any trouble with him. Then there was Aslin, Petty Officer Aslin, the senior of my staff of two. Aslin, who was with me from the beginning to the end, was a gift from the gods, a tremendous worker whom, even in those high-pressure days, I found I had to hold back sometimes. He dedicated himself entirely to his job, never took any leave, and yet was always tactful and cheerful. One meets these extraordinary men from time to time, I find, and I count it as one of my blessings that chance sent Aslin to me at a time when I desperately needed his extraordinary qualities.

The Clerget was a rotary, a new form of aero engine to this country, and one which at once caught my excited interest. The rotary had a number of advantages over the more orthodox in-line, radial or V-form engines. In a fighter the power/weight ratio, coupled with reliability, is everything, and the rotary was—and still is—the lightest form of piston aero engine for any given capacity. Because of this it is not necessary to force up the power output unduly with a high compression, and this of course gives it great reliability. At that time one of the rotary's advantages also created its own chief failing. The tip of a Clerget rotary was doing about 150 m.p.h. at cruising revs, and in order to reduce weight and centrifugal force loads the cylinders were finned and made of very thin steel. This was splendid for cooling one side of the cylinder, but the trailing edge, lacking the benefit of this airstream, became so hot that it caused distortion. The French got round this—or imagined they had—by fitting an obturator piston ring, which was rather like a leather washer in a bicycle pump, but made of a light alloy. It was very thin, very fragile and very unreliable; and when it broke the piston seized at once. They were giving a life of around fifteen hours in France, and this was an expensive way to try to gain air supremacy over the Western Front.

This wasn't the only trouble they were having at Gwynnes, and the realization that human lives were at stake began to worry my conscience soon after I arrived. It is amazing how easy it is to forget the responsibility you carry in a job far from the fighting line, involved in the day-to-day detail of your work and cushioned by the normal comforts of home life in the evening. So I was glad when the chance came to go out to France to see things at first hand; and that first visit certainly had a profound effect on my outlook, on my attitude to the war and to the men who were fighting it, on my work on the weapons we were providing them with, and I think, too, on the very fundamentals of my engineering philosophy.

The instructions I received were cryptic: we were losing far too many pilots through mechanical failures, and the cause was believed to be found in the wrist pins which were seizing up on the Clerget. I was to visit the squadrons near Dunkerque to investigate. I left Chiswick at once and arrived in France in a destroyer within a few hours.

This was the first of dozens of visits I made over the next three years. When the war began, there were two distinct and separately administered air arms, the R.N.A.S. and the R.F.C., under the Admiralty and War Office respectively. The factories, the story went, were split between the two by tossing a coin, and from the way things turned out this might even have been true. Anyway Gwynnes went to the R.N.A.S., nearly all of whose fighter and scout units were Clerget-powered in 1915; and it was to R.N.A.S. squadrons, stationed mainly between Ypres and Dunkerque, that most of my visits were made.

Feeling between the air arms was not too good and their relationship was soured by petty jealousies and rivalry that extended right up through the ranks and was nurtured by the false absurdity of the division. The R.N.A.S. squadrons seemed to me to be less smart, but they had better mechanics than the R.F.C., and on the whole I found them easier to work with.

Captain Charles Lamb was C.-in-C. of the R.N.A.S. overseas, a remarkably handsome, clean-cut man with iron-grey hair, whose H.Q. was at Marlo outside Dunkerque. In all my visits I found him consistently kind—almost fatherly—helpful and co-operative, and he never refused me anything for which I

askcd and always backed me 100% in any inter-departmental
tiffs. I never understood why everyone called him cold, severe
and difficult to approach (though all agreed that he was a
magnificent commander), and no one could understand why
he was so fatherly to me.

The formality of dinner in the mess with Lamb—an equally
handsome Alsatian dog at his side—was frequently broken by
shell-fire from a long-range German gun some twenty-seven
miles away.

Under Lamb was Frank McClean, a young Commander
and a less formidable and perhaps more cheerful figure than
his senior, who had virtually started the R.N.A.S. with his own
money some years earlier, when the Wright brothers were
considered mythical figures and Louis Bleriot's effort a fluke or
a fraud.

My trips always began at Marlo, and from there I travelled
out to the various R.N.A.S. squadrons, using our engines,
talking to squadron commanders, pilots and mechanics freely,
and getting at once from men who had just landed from
reconnaissance flights or dog-fights detail information on faults,
and sorting out possible cures on the spot. This wasn't simply a
time-saving convenience; the personal contact benefited both
sides, the pilots feeling that they were dealing with at least well-
intentioned and not entirely ignorant human beings instead of
frustrating bureaucratic machines, while I was all the better
for being (as I always was) frightened or moved—and always
impressed by the human element in our search for reliability
and performance.

Sometimes it was quiet enough at the airfields, and I
pulled engines to pieces, talked and drank, and was momentarily drawn into the squadrons' lives. At other times, when
perhaps the Germans or the Allies were thrusting forward
another few yards in some great offensive and the pilots were
flying three or four missions a day, it was sheer hell. There was
no romance about fighter work on the Western Front then,
with five from one flight spiralling down in flames without

parachutes, as happened on one visit; with grief, courage and
fear thrown together in hectic drunken parties among the
survivors in the evening; and with a fresh set of faces at every
airfield on every visit, the previous ones already as dim and
forlorn as in a fading group photograph. A visit to the
squadrons was a drastic and positive cure for any lurking
complacency.

I saw little of the fighting and was hardly ever in any real
danger, though once or twice I thought I was. I should have
gone on a bomber raid in a Handley-Page after dinner one
night if my machine hadn't been unserviceable. Instead I went
out in the moonlight to watch the others return, to meet a
storm of screaming bombs. The cunning Hun had mixed in
with our Handley-Pages and, guided by the landing-lights,
pasted us to such good effect that the squadron were reduced
to landing on the beach; a forerunner of the 'intruders' of the
1940s, proving again that there's nothing new in warfare!

There was often shelling, too. I was having a quiet cup of
tea outside with the Canadian fighter ace, Mulock, one afternoon, when every gun in Flanders seemed to open up on us.
Mulock, I noticed out of the corner of my eye, never stirred;
Big Bertha herself could have gone off under his deck-chair and
he wouldn't have spilt a drop. Then there was the occasional
strafing, which always set the place buzzing like a stirred-up
wasps' nest. The adjoining canal seemed to be the only retreat
left to me when a Fokker came over one day, and after a
terrific hundred-yard sprint with the bullets dancing behind
me, in I went with a splash and huddled under the overhanging
bank. The plane's next run across the airfield brought me
company in the shape of Petty Officer Clarke, and side by side
Bentley Motors' future head racing mechanic and I huddled
among the rushes, teeth chattering. The pilot who sent us
there, and helped to seal a warm friendship, was Baron von
Richtoffen himself. I almost felt a pang of regret when Brown
in a Camel, powered by one of our B.R.1s, caught him at last
a year or two later.

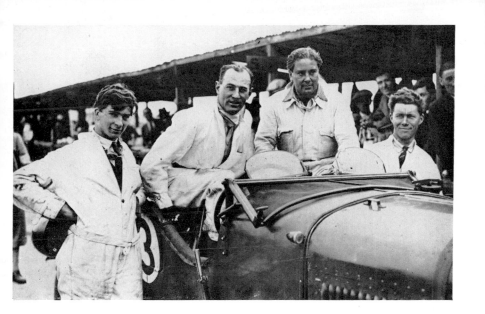

Above : Jack Dunfee and 'Babe' Barnato after winning the 1929 B.A.R.C.
Brooklands 6-hour race; Wally Hassan and Stan Ivermec stand by

Below : A line-up of 'Bentley Boys'. *Left to right :* Baron d'Erlanger, Barnato,
Birkin, Jack Dunfee, Kidston, Benjafield, Chassagne and Clement

Bertie Kensington
Moir tells a story

Babe Barnato seated, not in a stripped rear-engined Bentley, but in his
speed-boat, *Ardenrun*

I did fly sometimes, but, it appeared, never before they were assured there wasn't a Hun in the sky, and I was only really frightened once. This was on my first trip across the Channel, the one on which I was ordered because of the engine seizures, and which led up to this diversion from my account of the Gwynne factory.

Frank McClean took Aslin[1] and me to one of the squadrons having trouble with their Nieuports.

'Thank the Lord someone's doing something about this,' the C.O. greeted me. 'Flying the damn things is suicide.' He had already lost some of his best pilots so I could easily understand his abrupt manner.

We went off right away to work on one of the engines in the hangar, and after a few hours Aslin and I thought we had done the trick. I was wiping my hands on a bit of waste when the C.O. came up and asked us how we were getting on.

'I wouldn't mind going anywhere in this now,' I said wildly.

'Let's try and see then,' he said—without malice, even with a trace of merriment. 'You can go up on the dawn patrol tomorrow if you like.'

Some basic combat training would have helped in this situation, for I had never left the ground before, fired a shot in anger, nor even seen a Lewis gun, with which I was supposed to defend us from the roaming packs of Fokkers.

To the accompaniment of plenty of good-natured ribbing, I was instructed in the fundamentals of my weapon, dressed up like one of Scott's party, and put into the rear cockpit. We took off, turned into the rising sun, and made for the lines. I was convinced that the whole German Air Force was up there to meet us; the air was thick with planes, many of them under fire from anti-aircraft guns, and I prepared myself to swing the Lewis round on its scarf ring from side to side in defence against the inevitable diving attack. I will swear to this day that I

---

[1] Poor Aslin was the most sea-sick petty officer in the Navy. He survived two trips and then I took pity on him and left him behind.

F

really did spot a black-crossed Fokker, but before I could do anything about it my pilot swung away and we went out to sea.

I had plenty of time to think about the icy water 5,000 feet below, waiting to receive me if we had been slipshod in our work the night before. There was a very strong head wind, and we seemed to take hours to get back, and the rough landing nearly finished me off. I struggled out of the cockpit a shivering wreck, trying to assume an air of calm, while the pilots clustered round, uttering wisecracks.

All that was quite good fun-and-games, but there was nothing humorous about what I found when we opened up the engine to assure ourselves that all was still well. Three of the con. rods were blue from the heat—their life could be measured in minutes.

To me the consequences of that discovery were profound, and from then on the appalling sense of responsibility hung over me and never left me for the rest of the war, the figure of a pilot killed by engine failure leaning over my shoulder, like some ghostly conscience, whenever I was at work.

.   .   .   .   .

The routine at Chiswick was ceaseless and gruelling, and for months on end I returned home useless for any sort of social life, and a poor companion to my wife in the brief moments when I saw her. The only time I could detach myself from it all was on my drive to and from our house in Netherhall Gardens, Hampstead, in the 12–40 D.F.P. saloon: that one hour's tranquillity each day saved me from nervous exhaustion.

It would have been something if I could have reserved all my energies for engineering, but any engineer who has tried will tell you how impossible this is. In spite of the position of authority I occupied, I was soon neck-deep in the politics, manœuvrings and jealousies that arise when an outsider is let into the design department. I managed to persuade Gwynnes to raise the compression, and, because they were ordered to, they accepted the aluminium piston, but I met a series of carefully contrived obstructions when I tried to improve the obturator ring and incorporate a cylinder with good conductivity formed of aluminium with a cast-iron liner shrunk into it which would equalize the temperature. This, I was convinced, would solve the major unbalanced heating problem in a rotary engine. But at this stage I think Gwynnes thought they were being led into an entirely new design to my specifications, which would mean dropping the French Clerget rotary. Besides, they were also occupied with a new rotary of their own, for which they had brought over a designer from France.

Gwynnes would, in fact, rather drop me than their Clerget, and they made this so amply clear that I was forced to put my case to Briggs.

Briggs knew what I was after; he knew, even before my call, that I was anxious to get ahead with my own rotary design; but, as tactful as ever, he suggested that I should return to Chiswick, work on one piston and cylinder to my specification and fit it to a Clerget to prove my case. Both as an engineering and diplomatic proposition, this required patience and ingenuity, but the results were as satisfactory to me as they were disturbing to Gwynnes.

I won't dwell on the tiresome consequences of the experiment, but I was soon back at the Admiralty to ask to be removed from Chiswick and to be allowed to develop my own aero engine design elsewhere. I thought for a while that Briggs was temporizing, but he was only letting the clutch in slowly; soon the wheels were turning, and I was summoned back to his office and given my new orders.

'You're to take your bags to Coventry, Bentley,' he told me. 'Humbers have got all the facilities you'll want. They're only churning out Army bicycles—thousands and thousands of them —and terrible things like travelling kitchens. I think they're rather offended that they haven't been given something more challenging to test their mettle, so they'll welcome you with open arms.'

Briggs was right. Earl Russell, the Chairman (and Bertrand Russell's elder brother), Wright, in charge of the fitting shop, and Crundle, the chief tester, were bored stiff with the commonplace trivialities on their production lines and were delighted at the prospect of having an entirely new and exciting thing to get their teeth into. And so, of course, was Burgess, whom I had known in racing before the war. I was to have a lot to do with F. T. Burgess, head designer at Humbers—and draughtsman supreme. I soon recognized that we talked the same language, understood and appreciated the same things, and that he was a man in a thousand to have on design work. He had the most facile pencil of any man I have known, a pencil that flashed across the board in deft strokes, expressing in lines our ideas as quickly as the words were spoken. It was a wonderful sight to watch and the magic of it never failed to impress me, from those aero-engine days to the 'twenties when we worked together on the 3-, $4\frac{1}{2}$- and $6\frac{1}{2}$-litre Bentleys.

The other two with whom we were to be in close touch were the works manager, Niblett, a pleasant man who lacked only enthusiasm and what we considered a proper faith in rotaries; and Meason, the assistant works manager, a gay little live-wire of a man, bright, amusing and dead keen, about as strong a contrast to Niblett as you could imagine.

We settled down to work at once in the well-equipped drawing office, together with Aslin and his assistant, whom I had brought with me from Chiswick, and the first thing we did with our plans was to re-draw them. We were confident that the 120 × 160 mm. nine-cylinder rotary was ahead of anything the Germans had; but in war you've got to be two steps ahead of the enemy, and at that time our air supremacy on the Western Front was very much in the balance. The new design, which we intended should leap-frog the 120 × 160 mm., was basically similar but larger and more powerful, with an anticipated output of over 200 h.p. With the design completed, I went to Briggs with the drawings.

He looked at me doubtfully. 'You're asking to run before you've shown you can walk,' he said.

I used all my persuasive powers, certain that we should go the whole way, and I think he agreed with me. But he was thinking of 'their Lordships', who had consented only reluctantly and under pressure to allow me to make a start at all.

'Let's see the first one running, then I'll do what I can,' he told me.

There were no greater difficulties in the design of the larger than the smaller engine; they were fundamentally similar. If the fighter squadrons had received the first batch of B.R.2s[1] in early 1917 instead of 1918 it is even possible that the war might have been shortened. But that was not to be, and I went back to Coventry trying to console myself that I supposed we were lucky to have got the green light at all.

Harassed by Russell (as if we needed any spurring on!), we got the prototype on the test-bed by the early summer of 1916. Cracks were made later—which bothered me at the time—that the B.R.1 was an imitation Clerget. These originated from people who glanced only at the cam. mechanism, which of course was the first thing they saw and, for ease of production, was the only similar feature, and were probably incapable of differentiating even if they had bothered to look further. In fact the crank-case, crank-shaft, method of securing the cylinders themselves as well as their heads, were all fundamentally different from the Clerget.

We had the usual early setbacks but they were mercifully few. After watching one of the prototype's runs until I was ready to drop, I went home to the King's Head Hotel where I lived in Coventry. I understood later why we had so many complaints of noise from the factory, for on that night the B.R.1's roar seemed to fill the streets, and it followed me up to my room and hummed in my ears as I tried to go to sleep. I must have dozed off momentarily because the next thing I

[1] Bentley Rotary. It was earlier given the less unromantic tags, 'The Bentley' and 'The Admiralty'. The final order for B.R.2s was 30,000.

remember was sitting up with a start, suddenly aware of a horrible silence.

I was back at the works in a few minutes, to find that a valve had broken. I saw that the repair work was carried out and retired, only to be woken up again. Again it was that valve, which was lasting just three hours; and again I went back to bed, wondering what we could do to remedy this fault.

Once more I dragged myself from my bed that night, and this time it was a case of third time unlucky. There was a serious crack round the flange where the induction pipes were bolted on to the cylinder—a fault to be overcome but hardly one to justify Russell's horrified exclamation the next morning.

'I hear your engine's burst!' he greeted me.

'What on earth do you mean?' I asked. 'It's nothing that can't be fixed in a few days.'

Well, we did cure the trouble, and the valve failures were solved by considerably lightening them. There were no more snags, and the B.R.1 was ready for the Admiralty Inspector (none other than the helpful S. C. H. 'Sammy' Davis) by the late summer and in production by the autumn. Later we raised the compression so that the Camels got more speed at heights above 10,000 feet; and the only other modification we made originated from something of a mystery. One of the later experimental engines gave more power than it should have done, and after taking it to pieces and looking it over, we found a small leak in one of the induction pipes. Secretly, and feeling rather like vandals, we drilled a 2-mm. hole in the top casting of the induction pipe in another engine—and up went the power by 11 h.p. We sent the word round and fitters on every B.R. squadron were soon busy with little 2-mm. drills.

With the success of the B.R.1 proved, Briggs got authority for us to go ahead with the bigger unit without my having to ask him. It was a comparatively simple operation to get the prototype B.R.2 ready, the principle of the two designs being similar and many of the parts interchangeable. All this became too big for Humbers to cope with, so the Daimler factory was made the B.R.2 headquarters to co-ordinate the huge construction programme, and Crossleys, Humbers and several other firms all became involved. The B.R.2 was in production for the new Sopwith Snipes by the early spring of 1918, and output was running at more than 120 a week by the summer.

All through the development and testing period I tried to keep up my regular liaison visits to the squadrons. The pilots and mechanics still depended on these for passing on any grouses or suggestions, and though a few people tried to break up this irregular state of affairs, I always had Captain Lamb behind me, while Briggs turned the traditional naval blind eye. The only time I got into serious trouble was when I short-circuited the supply line.

I was over in France on 4 Squadron's airfield when I was horrified to hear that four of their aircraft had failed to return. Engine failure was suspected, and then news came in that two of the machines had come down in fields luckily on our side of the line—and two on the beach. I dashed off at once to the nearest one on the sands near Dunkerque and asked the discomfited pilot what the trouble was.

Actually the diagnosis was straightforward: the spring in the oil pump, which was made outside for us, was too hard and had broken under pressure. With the old phantom spurring me on, I raced back that afternoon, was at the factory in the evening, and—with the magnificent co-operation of the foreman and his men—had them at work on new springs by nightfall. They worked right through the night on correctly tempered substitutes, copper-plated for recognition, and I was away with a suitcase of them in time to catch the train back to Town and the morning destroyer. The men on the squadron thought I had pulled some sort of trick on them.

The row began when the accounts department at the Admiralty received an invoice for the springs which lacked the usual authority reference of the Admiralty Inspector, and then everything had to come out. A letter was followed by an interview; I was really on the mat, reminded that I was subject

to naval discipline, etc., etc. How had I got them over to
France? In a *suitcase*? What authority did I have to use the
destroyer, which was intended for . . .?

.   .   .   .   .

The great German last-fling offensive had expired and the
weight of the Allied blows was at last making cracks in the
enemy line. It was the summer of 1918; the B.R.2 was in full
production. Briggs had been superseded in the big upheaval
following the formation of the R.A.F., and his successor had
pinned his faith to a new air-cooled radial engine which was
intended to supplement the B.R.2 and had been put into hasty
production, so hasty in fact that there was urgent need for new
experimental work on it. I was asked to take over this post-
production experimental work at the factory.

The new radial engine, I discovered, caught fire easily, was
unreliable and ran far short on its power test at Farnborough.
I didn't like it, and told my new C.O. what I thought of it.

'Bentley,' he said, 'I think you're just tired. And in any case
it's natural for you to feel a certain prejudice.'

His first statement was all too true; the second made me so
angry that it's a wonder that I ever got out of his office without
committing violence.

That the war ended in November, before this radial
reached the squadrons in any numbers, was merciful; and that
my fears for it were realized gave me no satisfaction. It still
succeeded in killing several good men, among them the
brilliant test pilot, H. G. Hawker. His engine caught fire and
he went straight in.

I was sent on leave before the armistice and, after a last
tour of the squadrons, returned to Netherhall Gardens and my
wife, suffering a good deal from the reaction. I was still nomin-
ally a two-ringer (possibly the longest-serving junior officer
then, and certainly now, for I was never officially demobilized),
my personnel of only two disqualifying me from promotion.

That was all right, but the very low pay, on which I had to keep myself and a home going, had been a bit hard, and at one time I had had to appeal to Briggs for some assistance. The £1,000 tax-free gratuity he found for me helped things out, but no one could call me a war profiteer.

Money raised an uglier head two years later when I was invited to make a claim by the Royal Commission on Awards for the invention of the B.R.1 and B.R.2. My counsel was Douglas Hogg, K.C., later Lord Hailsham, and to back my case General Brooke-Popham and Sir William Brancker were there to give evidence to Mr. Justice Sargant and his Commission that the B.R.s were considerably superior to any other rotary used in the war and that it had improved both the strength and morale of the squadrons. Briggs was there to give support, too, and so were various other senior officers and much-decorated pilots. The opposition's claim was that, as a serving officer, I was merely carrying out my duties; and there was strong intervention from Gwynnes, too, who considered that they qualified for any award made as the original design had been conceived on their premises.

It was a beastly and tiresome business, the sort of situation at which I am not at my best, and after interminable delays I was granted £8,000—to the disgust of my counsel, who considered it such a niggardly pittance that he drastically reduced his fee, which would otherwise have about halved what I received. The last straw was the Inland Revenue's insistence that the claim was taxable, and this made me so angry that I determined to fight it. It was to be a test case, but a few days before it was due to be heard they capitulated. I was so disgusted by then that I don't think I even celebrated!

I had been married four and a half years but had seen very little of my wife during all this time. That her mother lived near her had helped, and when the Zeppelin bombing was at its worst (a high, steady barometer was an almost infallible indication of raids) I used to take the train down from Coventry in the evening, spend the night in Hampstead and return again in the morning. I now looked forward to some peace and quiet, and then with the war over—as it must be any day now—to preparing our plans for the formation of the company to produce the car we had been dreaming of for three years . . . even roughing out a few plans with Burgess as an occasional relaxation from the hurly-burly of rotaries at Coventry.

But if it held off its last blow for a few months, the war had not finished with me yet. Before my plans had materialized, before we had really got anywhere with our car, my wife died in the great Spanish 'flu epidemic that swept over shattered Europe.

6

EX 1

THE hospital matron was standing in the loft doorway, hands on hips, a formidable and displeased figure. 'Go and see what she wants,' I asked Gallop when I caught sight of her.

He came back in a few moments, a wry smile on his lips. Heaven knows how he had heard the indignant message he passed on to me through cupped hands: 'She says we're to stop this row at once. There's a man ill next door.'

'Tell her to go away,' I shouted back. What was the illness of one man? In here the birth of a new engine was taking place. 'A happy sound to die to—the exhaust roar of the first 3-litre Bentley engine!' someone remarked with awful irreverence later.

We gave it twenty minutes on the bench; then I told Nobby Clarke to switch off, and the gentle hum of traffic in Baker Street seemed a thousand miles away. Perhaps the poor man was really ill, though I fear my conscience wasn't struck till later. On that exciting morning in October, 1919, I had too many things on my mind.

.   .   .   .   .

On 20th January, 1919, Harry Varley, Burgess and I had sat down with nothing but a few bits of paper and some ideas in a small office on the top floor of a building in Conduit Street. There, to my instructions and to the accompaniment of endless technical talk, they had worked for nine months with hardly a break on the drawings of the design.

The seeds of it all had, of course, been sown during the

war when I had decided that it just wasn't going to be enough for me to return to the agency business, profitable though it had been, and would be again. The creative instinct is strong in most engineers, and, just as I hadn't been satisfied for long to work on someone else's rotary engine, so I had to produce my own car.

Briefly, and without getting too technical, what I had in mind was a bigger engine than the D.F.P.'s, which was a good and sound little unit, but there was a limit to how much you could push it; it was not, in fact, a natural power-giver. An engine with overhead valves, and enough of them, a capacity of 3 litres, would be about right, so that we should not have to force it too much to start with; a reliable unit which would require the minimum of maintenance and would stand up to long distances at high speed.

I had for a long time admired both the racing 3-litre Peugeot—one of the classic designs of all time—and the 1914 Grand Prix Mercedes engines. Both were natural power-givers; the Peugeot had two cam-shafts directly over each line of valves, with the plug in the centre, while the Mercedes had one cam-shaft running along the centre and the valves working through rockers and multiple plugs at the side of the head. The head was very well cooled, with water all round the valve seats and also round the plug bosses.

We approved of both these principles, except that we thought that the chain of gears driving the twin cam-shafts on the Peugeot would be a tricky proposition for the quiet running I thought was essential. I finally decided to go for a centre cam-shaft working the valves through rockers, with a bevel drive to the cam-shaft, and cast-iron cylinders, very open at the sides so that we could clear the sand away from beneath the exhaust valves.

People have asked me from time to time why we only had two-wheel brakes on the early 3 litres. The answer is that we didn't know enough about four-wheel brakes. Apart from racing, they had, I think, been used only on the Argyll, and until we had done some research on them we were afraid that the slightest unevenness in their application would affect the steering. But almost as soon as the car was in production we made enquiries of Perrot, who held the patents for what we considered a satisfactory front-wheel braking system, and it was his formula that we eventually used, a double differential looking after the compensation problem.

The market I had in mind for this car, which seemed likely to be as neglected as it had been before the war, was the fast sporting one. If the capital could be found, I thought we could meet it as successfully as we had between 1912 and 1914 with the D.F.P. The policy was a simple one. We were going to make a fast car, a good car, the best in its class; and when we had begun to show a profit and had obtained our own machine shop, then we would make a smaller, cheaper car—a bread-and butter car in fact as well.

Burgess, of course, I had known and worked with for years, and I have already told of his deftness and accuracy as a draughtsman. As hard a worker, as useful and with an even better theoretical knowledge, Harry Varley had been with Vauxhall and had done much good work there. These two worked on the drawing-board together, always efficiently, though later on perhaps rather less happily at times when their artistic temperaments got the better of them.

For several months Bentley Motors consisted of the three of us, while H.M. continued to look after D.F.P., making the money we were going to need. And he made a lot of it, about £20,000 in the first roaring boom twelve months after the armistice. Conditions were the same as they were in the late 1940s, with everybody wanting cars, everybody with money, and anybody who could turn out something with four wheels and an engine making it at a feverish rate. H.M. even had a relay of drivers working from the French factory, racing chassis as fast as they could go to the Channel ports.

This boom was all very nice, while it lasted, but it had an unsettling effect on us. It obviously couldn't last, and we wanted to be in on at least the tail end of it—which inevitably led to haste and frayed nerves. As we completed drawings for one part, so we had it made, a risky procedure we had to follow to save time. Anyone who has tried to make motor cars —or anything else for that matter—in boom times will know all about the frustrations and headaches involved in getting materials and in having anything made. With a four-year back-log to make up everyone had full order books, and there was hardly a factory in Britain seeking or even ready to welcome new customers. Here was our first difficulty. The second was not only much greater but almost inconceivable to anyone in the motor-car business today. We had to have *everything* made: gearbox, clutch, differential, bearings, stub axles—everything. There were no proprietary makes we could draw on, no ready-made back axles, no gear-boxes, no universal joints complete with cardan shaft and so on. To design and build a new motor car in 1919 without substantial capital was like being cast on to a desert island with a penknife and orders to build a house.

The only people we could get to help us were at a works in Bristol. A man there called Peter Purves was wonderful at getting our stuff through, whipping the bits out by a com-pound of zeal, determination and bullying so efficiently that we decided we must have him for ourselves. 'Come and bustle for us,' I asked him one day. 'As a sort of liaison officer.' And he agreed. Purves had all the right qualifications—diplomacy, the ability to mix well, and intelligence. He became the company buyer later and stayed with us to the end.

As things progressed we had to get in more help, and next came Clive Gallop on the design side. Gallop had fought in France with the R.F.C. as a pilot. He had driven at Brook-lands and—even more attractive to me—had worked for Peugeots. We had talked engines for hours in the past, in the same language and with identical enthusiasm, the first time on a train to the Midlands, and I think he had been half expecting the invitation I sent him in the summer of 1919. It was Gallop who helped to evolve the cam-shaft of the first 3 litre.

Jimmy Enstone was next, ex-Camel pilot, as Company Secretary, and then, with all the blueprints complete and most of the parts made, along came 'Nobby' Clarke. You'll remember our little flight from the Hun in the shape of the strafing Richtoffen when we took refuge neck-deep in the water of a French canal; but that wasn't the only occasion on which I had met Nobby. Number 4 Squadron, the first to get B.R.s, was my favourite, and I had had frequent contact with Petty Officer Clarke, the chief mechanic. It was as future head mechanic of Bentley Motors that I had kept my eye on him, and by a piece of happy telepathy or something, he wrote to me from his home in Kent. 'Why don't you call to see us?' I answered his letter of enquiry. 'We need someone to put this engine together.' By September he was doing just that in the loft above the D.F.P. service station in New Street Mews which we had then taken over, and doing it with all the skill and dexterity I had expected from him.

Thanks to high-pressure work and co-operation all round, that engine took shape with remarkable rapidity. There it sat on its roughly knocked-together bench, with its single magneto and large pre-war Claudel racing carburettor, all glinting aluminium and copper, and around it we all assembled, like the members of some sect drawn together to witness an ancient rite.

'Let's try and start it now,' I said to Gallop—and the manner in which it didn't has been told by others so I won't linger over the awful anxiety while Clarke tested the valve timing and fiddled with the carburettor. Benzole did the trick —and at once the three-inch exhaust was bellowing and the straight-tooth gears screaming with enough noise to awaken the dead. . . .

.   .   .   .   .

Well, we were over the first hurdle, but it was a long, long course. The next thing was to get the engine in a chassis and have the married pair ready to be presented at the first post-war Olympia Show in November. We even managed that, after a fashion. The gearbox turned up from Moss Gears, the rear axle, of banjo tubing, from the National Projectile Company, and so on. We tried to get the crank-case out of the Coventry firm who were making it, but they couldn't finish it in time and so we made do with a dummy. The cam casing was of wood, too, and though we had the valves in there was no valve gear. But it still looked quite impressive and created a lot of interest in spite of the fact that we were tucked away in a corner, and some of the more knowledgeable poked about rather embarrassingly. Today you could get away with a plywood shell for a motor car, but in those days a lot of people either knew or liked to pretend that they knew something about engineering, and you had to be prepared for technical questions.

That Show was a wild affair, with the hall packed all day, an atmosphere of abandon in the air as the crowds searched for something they could blow their money on. There were people begging to be allowed to put down as much as £200 deposit on the strength of our semi-mock-up: a sellers' market gone berserk. But we weren't having any of their money, badly as we needed it, until we had something more substantial to offer them.

Somewhat breathless as well as encouraged after all this, we took our precious Ex 1 back to New Street Mews, and then to the D.F.P. showrooms where, as our sole exhibit, it attracted more attention from passers-by in our window.

I thought until I started writing this book that I was the first person to take a Bentley on to the road, but it seems that I was wrong. Clarke tells of a precautionary move to ensure that all was well made by Gallop very early on the morning I was to take her out. There were no seats yet, and Clarke and Gallop packed themselves into a sort of cocoon of warehouse coats, and in some trepidation—and at some 3,000 r.p.m.—made their way out of the Mews into Baker Street in first gear, emitting an ear-splitting row into the still morning air. After a short interval

These are some of the cars I have owned or driven extensively: 12-50 D.F.P. record-breaker, Ex 1 the first 3-litre Bentley, 3-litre All-Weather, Weymann-bodied 6½-litre, 12-cylinder Lagonda, prototype 2½-litre Lagonda

Above : The honoured guest at the Savoy

Below : The elegant Cork Street showrooms in 1927

and with the car slowing perceptibly, passenger turned to
driver, to discover he had all but disappeared. Most of the
coats had wrapped themselves round the exposed prop. shaft,
and were about to be joined by Gallop himself. My drive,
however, was so uneventful that I can remember nothing at all
about it.

The noise was obviously one of the first things we should
have to do something about. Some people like it, and there are
apparently more of them about today than there were then,
but we weren't going to make our fortunes out of people who
liked noise; and in any case it offended me. The straight-tooth
gears and the scavenger oil pump were the chief culprits, and
for the production cars we decided to drop the dry-sump
lubrication and go over to orthodox wet sump, though this
wasn't altogether satisfactory either, and the 3 litre ended up
with a special tank separated entirely from the sump. We also,
incidentally, went over to a three-cam cam shaft with separate
exhaust rockers, added a second magneto, and swapped the
Claudel for a five-jet Smith.

Three hundred and sixty-seven days—and I record the
figure now with some astonishment—after Varley, Burgess
and I had our first session, *The Autocar* published its first road
test, a highly satisfactory one written in the unmistakable
style of 'Sammy' Davis. Besides the richly effective but not
altogether relevant adjectives and classical analogies regarding
'speed' in general, the handling, the brakes, the comfort, and
especially the sheer performance, were all highly praised, and
the noise from the oil-pump drive was forgiven as a fault
'inseparable from the first chassis of a new design'. It stretched
over two pages and there were three impressive photographs.
How I wished we had had the cars we could have sold a dozen
times over as a result of that piece of publicity!

What we probably ought to have done at this stage was to
turn out three prototype chassis and use these to find someone
to capitalize adequately a new company. Production might
then have gone ahead from a properly equipped works where

G

we could have been self-supporting instead of dependent—as we always were—on outside firms. Perhaps that boom can be blamed for our decision to go ahead on our own, struggling for a dozen years to show the profit necessary before we could go to the public and form a public company. We were greedy, I suppose, or perhaps too independently minded. An entire chapter of this book could be written about our financial crises; instead you will find them cropping up like festering boils all through this Bentley Motors period, just as they racked us persistently for twelve years with hardly a moment of peace.

H.M. was at that time trying to get the finances on to some sort of footing that would make it possible for us to build or buy a works, for all we had so far were the drawing-offices in Conduit Street and the little place in New Street Mews. I think almost everyone thought that these ought to be somewhere in the Midlands, where we should be in close touch with the supplying firms on whom we were to be dependent, but I wasn't having that. Put it down to prejudice if you like, and I think my decision was probably a wrong one, but I was insistent that London should be our headquarters—if we could find the right place. This didn't prove easy, and in the end we were reduced to buying a plot of land in Oxgate Lane, Cricklewood, a plot near the Welsh Harp, bordered at that time by fields and rolling countryside, and on this we erected a small brick building for the assembly of the next three experimental cars.

The year 1920 was one of some development and much frustration when a deuce of a lot of money went out and none at all came in, and the soft sales situation began very slowly to harden as we were forced to increase our overheads. To build those first cars we had to take on more labour, and more mechanics at Cricklewood meant that we had to have a works manager, while our new experimental department again required someone to manage it.

If we had more than our share of bad luck in those early

days, and if we made more mistakes than we ought to have
done, we were at least blessed by exceptionally good staff.
R. S. Witchell, works manager for the entire life of Bentley
Motors, was another R.F.C. man, and I have already told how
I met him before the war, and was at school with him at
Clifton and later dashed up many a hill after his Straker-
Squire. Everybody respected Witchell, and there was never
during all his time any labour trouble; he was an ideal man for
the job, sound, steady and completely fair-minded. He and
Frank Clement, with his light-hearted, devil-may-care attitude
to life, made a strongly contrasting but a surprisingly well-
matched pair. Clement, too, had been with Straker-Squire,
and his racing experience was at least the equal of Witchell's.
He looked after the experimental department, later helped on
the testing and sales side, and was, of course, always our
Number One professional driver.

Then there were the mechanics whom Clarke took on,
nearly all as boys: Stan Ivermee, who was to follow me to
Rolls-Royce, then to Lagondas, and is now with Bristols;
Jack Sopp, one of this country's greatest racing mechanics
today; Wally Hassan, now a distinguished engineer; Saunders,
father and son; Jackson, Puddephat, Howard, Martin, Pryke,
and others, all loyal and first-class men, and a credit to Clarke's
talent for selection. The young Lord Settrington, today the
Duke of Richmond and Gordon, and, besides one of Britain's
greatest landowners, a vigorous supporter of motor racing,
came along later to the service station as an ordinary mechanic.
It was the only way to learn the engineering business, he
sensibly decided, and after we agreed that he should work
under an assumed name, he turned up conscientiously with the
other men at eight o'clock every morning. It was a long time
before rumours began to circulate around the works, and the
first suggestion that his secret was out came to him when he
was prostrated on the oily floor under a 3-litre's differential.
' 'Ave you 'eard, Charlie?' he overheard. ' 'Ear there's a bloody
Lord in 'ere.'

A drawing-office went up at Cricklewood in the autumn, and Varley and Burgess moved into it. The offices were alongside, and now we began to look around for some showrooms— just in case, one day, we should have something to show in them. Hanover Street had brought us fortune in the past and it seemed a good omen when we took a lease on excellent premises there. Showrooms demanded a sales organization as well as something to sell, and here we had a small ready-made unit—again thanks to D.F.P. With our expansion, H.M. had sold the concession (and just in time, for the French firm went bust soon after), and we had his salesmen ready and willing to shift their loyalties to the new *marque*. A. F. C. Hillstead, an excellent salesman who could drive so beautifully that he could have sold a lorry as a limousine to a duchess, became sales manager under H.M.; and under him was a nice young man called Hugh Kevill-Davies, who had had a tough time as a P.O.W. for most of the war, and was to become one of the most successful car salesmen in the country.

That was the line-up in the summer of 1921, and on the whole it was a satisfactory one. Later on the inevitable little personal differences would inevitably show themselves, leading to the occasional resignation, and there were to be some difficulties in the sales-production-design relationship. For the present, however, we had no cars over which to disagree, and the single-minded aim—to get them on the market—united us.

.   .   .   .   .

One morning in September, 1921, a tough, smart, short-set young man turned up at the works. I went out to meet him, and took him over to the low 3-litre coupé that was standing waiting for him. 'Let us know if anything goes wrong, Noel,' I said to him. 'You've got a five-year guarantee, don't forget.' He looked the car carefully all over, raised the bonnet and cast an experienced eye over the engine, got into the driving seat and drove away. Our first customer had taken delivery of our first production car.

The choice of this first customer was a tricky and important one. He would naturally be sympathetic to the sort of car we were producing or he wouldn't be paying over £1,000 for his model. But he also had to be something of a social butterfly who would mix in the best social strata and spread the good word far and wide, and something of an engineer who could appreciate the qualities of his car, talk about them authoritatively, and come back to explain any snags to us.

Noel Van Raalte was very rich. He owned Brownsea Island, among his properties, and put up the money for K.L.G. plugs. He was very sociable. And besides his excellent mechanical knowledge, he had also had racing experience, which had begun while he was still an undergraduate, when he had taken part in those memorable races in reverse gear round the streets of Cambridge, in a Grand Prix Mercedes.

If there were any weak spots in our car, we were confident that they would show up in the hands of Van Raalte. I thought he would make an excellent testing and propaganda tool.

Everybody went back to work feeling encouraged and much more hopeful about the future. Inside, six more chassis were nearing completion.

7

RACING AS A POLICY

IF THERE was one subject on which we never had any argument through all the crises and storms of Bentley Motors, through disagreeable board meeting after disagreeable board meeting, it was on our racing programme. Directors and chairmen came and went, sometimes at a bewildering rate, but, even when I was no longer managing director, I remained in control of the racing side of the business. No one ever attempted to dispute that competition success was the cheapest way of selling cars—and how could they? Time and again we got front-page lead headlines and as much as 200 column inches in the daily Press for one race, and even in our most active and successful year, when we couldn't put a foot wrong, the racing side cost us less than £2,500.[1]

The racing policy—as soon as we could afford one—was a part of the very foundations of Bentley Motors, for the two vital purposes of testing and publicizing our cars, and as you will see later, there is nothing contradictory in the fact that we were successful in both roles and yet still failed to survive; though I will be the first to agree that there is an important lesson to be learned in this apparent contradiction. Pre-war racing with D.F.P. had been a useful training ground, and the war years, and especially the months between the armistice and the production of Ex. 1, had given me the chance to formulate my general ideas on racing. These altered from time to time but

---

[1] The figures for 1924–5 to 1928–9 were £833, £2,412, £3,369, £2,616 and £2,487, after allowance had been made for prize and starting money, and manufacturers' and fuel and oil companies' bonuses. During the same period the money spent on Press advertising varied from between two and five times this amount.

remained basically the same, and perhaps I should put them down here and now in their simplest terms for the record.

First, we never entered for a race (except for the '22 T.T. trial effort) unless we thought we would win, and if we won we liked to do so at the lowest possible speed in order to preserve our cars and keep our true maximum performance from our competitors. We were in racing not for the glory and heroics but strictly for business, and sprints, 'garden-party' affairs round little circuits, handicap events on winding circuits without a decent straight on which we could take advantage of our superior speed, were all out. A small car can go round a corner as fast as or faster than a large car, which is all too often baulked by the babies—unintentionally of course—on winding or narrow roads. What sort of use could these races be to us? The Ards T.T.s, with their complicated handicapping, in which we never entered officially, proved our point exactly, for only once were they won by a big engined car.

In later years, when we were getting all the publicity we could ask for, this policy became more inflexible, for we knew only too well that the news that Bentleys had lost—or had crashed or blown up—would take precedence even over the announcement of the winning car. 'Bentley *Doesn't* Win' became a sort of nightmare headline to me, underlining the hideous consequences of possible failure!

The Brooklands 500-mile and Double-Twelve races were just right. And so, of course, was Le Mans, with its long straight, and the advantage it gave a comparatively large engine which has not been unduly pushed. Again the results proved our point: time and again at Le Mans cars have finished in descending order of engine size, as in the most recent (at the time of writing) when it was 3.4, 2.9 and 2.5 litres respectively. We got such a hold on the Sarthe race that by degrees we succeeded in driving out the opposition, the most successful and economical way I know of winning a race, and one which, because the engines were so little stressed, sometimes eliminated the need to take them down afterwards, though Clarke nearly always did so just to satisfy himself. I would have been perfectly content to see our cars circulating round Le Mans in inglorious solo solitude so long as the *Daily Mail* gave us their front page on Monday morning!

The second formula for success: sound, painstakingly meticulous preparation. 'Everything split-pinned, nothing too much trouble' might have been our motto. Clarke never let us have a car until he had been over it personally, end to end, inside and out, and when a man of his temperament had done his job, the drivers could feel that vital confidence in a machine on which their lives were to depend for a long time.

As to the drivers, we were fortunate in always having a mile-long waiting list which included the best amateurs of the day. The final choice for the team was always mine, and I was looking for drivers who were fast and steady and untemperamental, who would do as they were told, and who, if they didn't win and bring us the publicity, would survive to the finish to fulfil our second requirement and provide us with the evidence of any faults or weaknesses.

Next in importance I would put our pit-work, as applied to drivers and mechanics. Fast, efficient pit-work giving an advantage of three-quarters of a minute over a near rival (and we did better than that sometimes) could represent a saving of more than a mile and cause just that extra strain on your rival in attempting to make good the loss that could blow up his engine. I'll have more to say about our methods later.

We started off quietly and tentatively, using Ex. 2, a nine-foot chassis with a two-seater body, and with Frank Clement, the obvious choice, as driver. He had been using Brooklands for months for testing and had already put up speeds of over 90 m.p.h. with the fully equipped car when we took it down for the 1921 Essex Car Club and Whitsun meetings in May, and got a fairly comfortable first in one of the races. But we still had far too much to do, and far too little money, for there to be any sort of programme yet, and we did nothing further that year.

Oddly enough the famous American Indianapolis 500 miles was the first major event in which we entered; it was also our first major error. It was an expensive business sending the professional driver, Hawkes, and a mechanic with the car across the Atlantic, but apart from the usual intention of winning, we were anxious to show the Americans what we were doing. So far as the race went, we just weren't fast enough, but we finished, which was more than a lot of the cars did, and we created quite a good impression. Indianapolis had been won once or twice by European cars, but it was becoming too specialized a race for anyone but experienced natives to stand a chance in it, and it has in fact been almost an all-American affair ever since.

The same reasoning that had led us to enter the little D.F.P. for the 1914 Tourist Trophy race decided us now to put in a full team for the 1922 Isle of Man event, the first one since the war. In 1914 we had stolen much of the winning Sunbeam's thunder by keeping ahead of a lot of bigger cars and finishing, one of the six survivors out of twenty-three starters, 'among the big boys'. This time we hoped to do the same thing by finishing, as a team, as the only genuine 'touring' cars in a field consisting entirely of specially built 3-litre racing cars. If we won—then that would be splendid. But our primary motive was to put the cars in the public eye and get them talked about.

Early in the year, Clement took over four of the production chassis from the works and began working on them in the experimental shop. Modifications weren't to be elaborate, but they were to be carried out with infinite care: high-compression pistons, a racing carburettor, an outside exhaust system, and a smaller, flat radiator. The two-seater body was as non-standard as it was unlovely, with the spare wheel concealed in the 'streamlined' tail. But they were our first-team cars and we were proud of them.

We had sent a similar car over for the Indianapolis 500

on 30th May; as the T.T. was on 22nd June it was touch-and-go whether Hawkes would get back in time, and he only just made the first practice.

The Manx circuit hadn't changed much in the eight years since I had last driven on it; it was still very rough, with constantly changing surfaces, each, it seemed, with lower skid-resisting properties than the last, a riotous variety of corners and narrow, hump-backed bridges, and a road width that often appeared to be endangering all four hub caps simultaneously against the island's dry-stone walls. But what fun it was, especially that sweep down from the mountains, sometimes breaking out of cloud like a diving aeroplane!

There weren't so many familiar faces among the bars and hotel lounges of Douglas as there had been in 1914. Four years of war was one cause; another was the curious nature of the race, which permitted out-and-out racing cars with a capacity limit of 3 litres when the International Grand Prix formula limit was 2 litres. Entries for this odd-race-out were consequently sparse, and I doubt if there would have been any at all if it hadn't been an international event carrying with it some prestige and tradition. De Hane Segrave, the French professional, Chassagne, and 'Bill' Guinness were there as the official Sunbeam drivers, along with *le patron* himself, Louis Coatalen. Then there were M. C. Park, Payne and Swaine, the Vauxhall drivers, non-competing drivers of varying eminence, and two whose future fortunes were later to be tied up closely with Bentley Motors.

One of these was the Marquis of Casa Maury, an international sportsman, a dark, dashing gentleman of pleasure and business, of Colombian origin I think, who was later to become the company's joint managing director and to follow our racing programme with keen personal interest. He was down to drive one of the leaping fleet little Bugattis in the 1,500 c.c. Trophy that was to be run off simultaneously with the T.T. in order to fill out the thin field, and he did very well in it, too, coming in third behind the Talbot-Darracqs of 'Algy' Guinness

and Divo, and only 6 m.p.h. slower than the winning Sunbeam
in the main event.

I don't remember meeting Maury in Douglas; but if I had
never met Bertie Kensington Moir again I would always have
remembered my first conversation with him. Bertie served
Bentley Motors with distinction, at the wheel, in the pits, and
in the service station, though the T.T. was all over and we
were on our way home in the *Castle Mona* when we were
introduced and exchanged drinks. Bertie, with his vast good
humour, his ebullience and warm, generous heart (aside from
his storehouse of tales, false and true), is a person one never
forgets. We talked about our experiences of the day before,
when Bertie had had fun with the famous Aston Martin,
'Bunny', in the 1,500 race before a valve put him out, and we
talked clear across the Irish Sea, through the night and through
quite a few more drinks.

In the cold light of dawn on Liverpool docks I asked him if
he would like to join us.

'I think that would be a very good idea,' he said, obviously
delighted at the idea.

The I.O.M. T.T.s were usually pretty wet affairs, but I
think 1922 was the wettest of them all, and we all knew we
were in for an uncomfortable ride, in spite of the three-ply
mudguards we had wired above the front off-side wheels. Park
was the first away at half past nine in a Vauxhall, followed by
Clement with Sanders as riding mechanic in Number One
Bentley, and Segrave. I was fifth off, with Pennel crouching
down beside me in the passenger seat. Almost at once the floorboards of my car worked loose, making the unspeakable discomfort of the rain seem almost insignificant, and before the
lap was out—a lap in which I somehow managed to go faster
than all the Vauxhalls and the other Bentleys—the floor was
no more. Try it one day, driving for a mile or two with your
feet supported solely by the control pedals. You'll see what I
mean by its being hard work; and I had five more hours ahead
of me.

Just to cheer me on, Simon Orde, a friend of Clement's who was managing our pit, chose that moment to hang out the faster sign for me. I was so cross that I got the sulks and never glanced at the pit again until the end of the race, which caused me to lose third place by 6 sec. to a Vauxhall: the warning that he was closing was there for me to see and I had plenty of reserve in hand, but I never glanced at it. Later on in the race most of the giant outside exhaust broke loose, nearly gassing and roasting Pennel, and for some reason giving us additional silence. Altogether it was quite a race.

Clement put up a very good performance in Number 3 and was only four minutes behind Chassagne at the finish, while Hawkes, who lost his plug and all his water early on—and caused a sensation in the grandstand when he added cold water to a red-hot radiator—pulled well up again and came in fifth, which secured for us the team prize.

The T.T. was an introductory—an experimental race if you like—for us, and the results were very pleasing. We issued a rather splendid brochure afterwards, full of photographs and impressive statistics to show potential customers that in the 3 litre they had a car that could be as docile as a limousine and yet could also compete on equal terms with the fastest stripped racing cars of the day. We then offered the three team cars for sale, and they went in a flash, at very satisfactory figures.

.   .   .   .   .

The T.T. result and the excellent publicity we had received from it cheered up the board and made things almost pleasant for me at the next meeting. I can see now why I dreaded these monthly board meetings, why I always found them so uncomfortable and resented the loss of time from what I considered the real work; and why I was a good deal to blame for the unhappy atmosphere that hung over them.

Money in life, as they say, is a great comforter, and nowhere does this worn platitude apply more strongly than at company board meetings. I am not exaggerating when I say that we never gathered together at Hanover Street with feelings of confidence in the financial position. Usually we were deep in a crisis, and often it was so critical that we had to face the total inability to pay the following week's wages. That is the first thing to remember about board meetings.

The quality of the board was the next factor. Because we were always under-capitalized in those early days, we were not in a position to pick and choose our directors, and some whom we persuaded to invest in our motor car were sharp men with improbable backgrounds, who were totally out of touch with the car business in general and our sort of car business in particular, with its emphasis on reputation and long-term customer goodwill. Cars are still booming, there's money in cars, let's build cars—any old cars will do—quickly: that was the attitude of many of them, and of course any sort of get-rich-quick policy was totally alien to our way of thinking.

After a few rows of varying degrees of unpleasantness, most of this riff-raff became impatient, demanded their money back and got out. We weren't sorry to see them go; our fault, I suppose, lay in not being able to pick and choose more selectively and in some way in being out of touch with the more solid sources of capital in the City and in the accepted Midland motor area.

A man called Boston was our first chairman, but he lasted only until the minor depression of 1923 (which of course hit us particularly hard just when we were getting the first chassis on to the market), when Stuart de la Rue took over. He owned the famous playing-card firm, which also printed bank notes and sundry other things on a large scale, and had a great deal of money. He came in, like so many of the really useful men, because of his interest in cars, especially our sort of car: a small, florid, fiery little man, and a real enthusiast in everything he took up.

W. S. Keigwin was one of the more helpful of the early directors, a society man who was very useful at introducing the

right sort of customer, but not always quite so sound at finding
the right sort of people to put up money, a task to which he
applied himself industriously. Guy Peck, who had been with
de la Rues, and subsequently with the Aircraft Manufacturing
Company, became an admirable general manager.

As a working director and head of the service department,
when we got that side going, there was Hubert Pike, who came
in early and stayed right to the end, proving an absolute boon,
always getting on well with the customers and establishing
himself as a vital link between us and them. I still have an
enormous folder of customers' letters, many of whom have a
special word of praise for their reception at the service station
from Pike, and his second-in-command, Bertie Moir. Pike had
been at prep school with me, had been at Humbers during the
war, and afterwards had had a D.F.P., so our association was
already particularly close. Pike was also adept at finding
capital, but I remember him with especial warmth as the man
who used to make my speeches for me at those tedious (and to
me intimidating) business functions.

These, and several others whose names I have now forgotten, I remember with warmth and affection from those
trying early years. Most of the others I prefer to forget, especially the gentleman whose departure we would gladly have
hastened if we could have afforded to, who suggested as a
condition of continued support that he should take a substantial commission on each car our sales department sold.
Drastic retribution for this blackmail came to him on the
Stamford–Grantham road one night when he drove flat out
into the rear of a stationary lorry.

A natural corollary to our uncertain capital position was
the question of overheads and expenditure. I was determined
that when we bought machinery and equipment for the works,
experimental and service departments, then it should be of the
very best; bearing in mind the motor car and the reputation
we were attempting to build, any other policy would have been
folly. But there were always those who would niggle and nag,

demanding economies, constantly pressing for the second-rate for a car we were to advertise and sell as the finest in its class, opposing the expenditure of money on vital equipment. There was one early and particularly sharp exchange over the purchase of a dynamometer when we were assembling the experimental chassis. Here we were, building a high-quality, high-performance sports car, and we were expected somehow to manage without any instrument with which to measure the horse-power! This was the sort of silliness that irritated me beyond endurance.

The trouble was that Bentley Motors was everything to me. All my ambitions were contained in that car, and the designing, building and perfecting of it were my whole life, occupying all my waking thoughts and every minute of my days. In those critical formative years of the company, when the loss of my wife still lay heavily on me and there was no gentle cushion of domesticity to support me and absorb the shock of the reaction after a hard day's work, I am sure I was not easy company. I was taciturn, unresponsive and over-sensitive to criticism, and in the intimacy of the board room these characteristics became more marked and I was at my worst.

Normally if I was cross, dissatisfied with something, or if I disagreed with someone, I might either mutter inaudibly or express myself in total silence, all of which was perfectly understood by the men at the works; I hated rows and violent words, which were nervously exhausting and took your mind off your work. Unfortunately I couldn't do this in board meetings; I was supposed to talk and explain and justify, feeling all the time I was being forced to make excuses for myself and others when I felt that none was required, begging for things which should have been offered, always on the defensive, a situation I detest.

And all the time was the feeling that I was letting down the works people, who were crying out for equipment and material and facilities to do their job better. Nor were matters helped by the fact that I was the only director with any engineering qualifications, and in the final issue the board was therefore obliged to accept my word : an unhealthy situation.

As time went on we got into the inevitable dilemma of any company dependent on outside firms for its supplies which becomes more and more seriously behind in its payments to them, and more and more at the mercy of the few who will continue to extend credit. We got seriously into the hands of the people who supplied us with our raw materials, who at one time were squeezing us so tightly that we lost all strength to argue, being forced to accept ever higher quotations as the price of continuing supplies. This was the sort of subject on the agenda that made me dread and detest board-meeting days.

I may be giving the impression that meetings of directors of Bentley Motors in the early days were unremitting shouting matches, which would not be true. There were always many routine matters of a day-to-day nature to be discussed, on which I was as silent as possible, my thoughts, I confess, often far away on current technical problems.

8

THE BENTLEY CUSTOMER

WITH the D.F.P. we had proved that there was an enthusiastic public willing to pay well for the privilege of speed, good handling, and also perhaps the distinction of ownership that that French car provided. I said earlier that the market we had in mind for the Bentley was the fast, sporting one. We were confident that if we could sell a good many slightly tuned French family cars on the strength of their performance and pleasant handling qualities, then the marketing of an open high-performance quality car should not present too many difficulties. All cars were selling easily when we began, and of course there were far more young and youngish men with money thirty-five years ago than there are now. The competition within our range was negligible. We were, in fact, though we didn't know it at the time, starting a cult which had a certain parallel in the United States in the early 1950s. It would be an absurd over-simplification to say that the Bentley initiated the sports-car tradition in this country; but I think it is true that, because we specialized exclusively in the manufacture of high-performance cars, because our racing successes received more publicity than those of any other make of car, the name of Bentley became so closely identified with the term 'sports car' that they became popularly synonymous.

The romantic association of the car with speed, the constant references to it in the Press and as the normal transport of fictional heroes from Bulldog Drummond to Ian Fleming's *James Bond* of today, all helped to create the false impression that the Bentley was the only sports car, so that any fast, open machine was popularly thought of as a Bentley, and anyone driving one as rather dashing.

The Bentley creed is a vast field for exploration for the social historian studying the 'roaring 'twenties'. I am not here concerned with sociology, nor am I concerned with the respective merits of the Bentley and its competitors, but only with the curious fact that the Bentley car, the Bentley Boys, the Bentley tradition, actually came to represent in the minds of many something of the very spirit of a decade.

However, in 1923 we were still little known, struggling furiously with the problem of making the cars as well as of selling them, and with neither the time nor the money to consider a full competition programme. Our customers were mostly sporting industrialists and business men, with a sprinkling of rich society young men, such as the very young Prince George, who had had a D.F.P. and came along and exchanged it (with the balance in cash) for a 3 litre, the first of many transactions we had with him.

Later, when our clientele expanded, our register began to look like an anthology of *Debrett* and the *Directory of Directors*. Tallulah Bankhead, Gertrude Lawrence, Beatrice Lillie all had Bentleys, and it became almost a routine for visiting American film and stage stars—and many Eastern potentates and European royalty too—to go home with one. Jack Buchanan was one of our staunchest supporters and had the very first production 8 litre, the Prince of Wales a 4½ saloon.

We were then producing a chassis for an open two- or four-seater body, and at first our customers were of the rugged, open-air-loving type to whom you would naturally expect to sell this kind of car. But it wasn't long before disturbing things began to happen and we heard of people putting on impossibly heavy closed bodywork for which the chassis was never intended. We never thought of the 3 litre as a closed car, and certainly not as a town carriage, and this was the function for which some misguided people were using it, in spite of its four-cylinder engine and the vibration, particularly on the over-run, which soon set up rattles in the clumsy and elaborate saloon bodywork of the time.

To extend the chassis beyond its original 9 ft. 9½ in. to 10 ft. 10 in. in order to accommodate a roomier body and closed coachwork was an unnatural distortion of the design, which would certainly lower the performance. But this was what we were forced to do under pressure from the sales people, who were only reflecting the public's requirements. I regarded this purely as a stop-gap arrangement before we could get down to the design of a six-cylinder car with a greater engine capacity to fill the role adequately. Already, you see, we were having to adjust our policy to meet the taste of our customers, and to expand our clientele. By the autumn of 1923 we were listing, besides the two-seater and four-seater Speed Models on the original short wheel-base and for the first time with the red enamel background to the radiator badge, five forms of standard bodywork on the long chassis, ranging from the open four-seater at £1,225 to the four-door Double Saloon, with seats for seven, at £1,415, which was an imposing-looking vehicle if you like, but very distant from the original conception of the Bentley we had formed four years earlier.

We could afford little on advertising in those days; for our goodwill and reputation we were dependent on the recommendations of our customers and agents and distributors, and on the whole we were singularly fortunate in these. The personal enthusiasm of our customers, who felt that in buying a car they had established a personal stake in the firm, who would visit us at the works and service department for long technical discussions, was remarkable. We owed a tremendous debt for the good word they spread in conversation and by practical demonstration of the car in competition.

I suppose the person to whom we owed most was John Duff, a young enthusiast who had been born in China and had established himself as one of our London agents. Duff, a man with tremendous guts and determination, had bought a standard short-chassis 3 litre, had done some work on the

engine himself, stripped off the wings and taken it to Brooklands to chase the D-class records. Driving single-handed on
the 28th September, 1922, he had comfortably taken everything from the Three-Hour to the 1,000 miles at speeds of
around 88 m.p.h., which did us a lot of good.

A few months later he called in at Hanover Street and told
H.M. and Hillstead that he had heard that the French were
planning a race at Le Mans to run for twenty-four hours and
that he wanted to enter.

H.M. passed the information on to me. 'He wants us to
back him, prepare the car, provide him with a mechanic and
co-driver, and generally give him our blessing,' he told me.
'What do you think?'

'I think the whole thing's crazy,' was my comment.
'Nobody'll finish. Cars aren't designed to stand that sort of
strain for twenty-four hours.' That was what I thought of Le
Mans.

But Duff was a very persuasive man who was used to
getting his way. Finally we agreed that Clement's experimental department should help prepare his 3-litre tourer for
the race, and that Clement himself and Saunders and Bezzant
should go over to Le Mans with him. No other British manufacturer was supporting the event, and I thought they were
probably very wise; I viewed the whole thing with the gravest
suspicion.

The race was on a Saturday, the start four in the afternoon,
as it is today. By Friday morning I was already in a fever of
anxiety and suffering from a very bad conscience, and in the
afternoon I could stand it no longer. In spite of the promise I
had made myself, I drove over from the works to Hanover
Street, where I found Hillstead.

'Come on,' I told him. 'We've got to go and see this stupid
race. We'll take the night boat.'

He was delighted at the prospect even though we had to
travel by train, turning up at Le Mans at midday, a few hours
before the start, and to the great surprise of Clement and Duff.

After a few hours in the pit I decided that this wasn't at all stupid; that it was, in fact, very exciting. Before darkness fell and the acetylene arc lamps at the corners were turned on, Le Mans was beginning to get into my blood. By midnight, with the cars pounding past the stand with their lights on—my first sight of racing in the dark—I was quite certain that this was the best race I had ever seen.

The rugged course with its long straights exactly suited the Bentley, and though the rough, rain-sodden surface had caused Clement to lose one of his headlamps, he was well up in the field against the strong opposition of a lot of 5.3-litre Excelsiors, 3.5-litre Lorraines and 3-litre Chenard et Walckers. There was no sleep for me that night, and at daybreak Duff was running a good second until he overdid things at Mulsanne. However, Clement made up for that by breaking the lap record several times, finally setting it at 66 69 m.p.h. Another flying stone intervened at this point—it's difficult for the racing driver of today to imagine what a menace they were—and punctured the Bentley's fuel tank. The announcement of this mishap was treated by the French as a great joke, it being the stock excuse for mechanical failure, and Duff's panting arrival at the pits was roundly and ironically cheered. However, they were quite prepared to accept the truth and respond with genuine cheers when Clement dashed off on a bicycle with a couple of cans, brought the car to the pits, and succeeded in mending the hole by the time-honoured chewing-gum method.

I was never more surprised and delighted than when we came in fourth in that first somewhat casual and slap-happy effort.

. . . . .

The only relaxation I ever had during the entire Bentley Motors period that remotely resembled a holiday was on Continental tests of the cars. In these extended runs all over France, up and down the passes to test the cooling and at high speed for hundreds of miles at a stretch, I could combine my love for travelling over great distances with something that was useful.

I put up huge mileages in those years, so that I think it is reasonable to claim that I drove every model of our cars farther than anyone else; at the wheel I could not only beat out from the car any possible troubles, but I also found it the most fruitful place to think out the answers to them. On the first 8 litre, years later, I once drove from Dieppe to Cannes in the day, without having to switch on the lights, cruising at around 85 m.p.h. for hour after hour by myself, chewing a few apples and sandwiches on the way. That was memorable motoring.

It was as a result of these trips that I became the Francophile I am today. I learnt from France that there was such a thing as a sun that rises and sets in a cloudless sky day after day, to refresh me, fill me with new vigour—and burn me to a nice shade of nut brown. I also learnt to love the free, friendly, classless people, their chateaux and cathedrals, their towns and hotels, and food and wine. I have always been too busy (or lazy) to learn their language properly, but I love it all the same, and can even be temped into talking it, so long as there are no other English people around. My idea of heaven has always been to take a car across the Channel and drive along those incomparable roads to the south—and the Mediterranean sun.

The first test run took Hillstead and me conveniently to Tours, a few days after Le Mans, where the French Grand Prix was taking place; so we can both claim to be among the few English people to have witnessed the only major Grand Prix to be won by an Englishman in a British car.[1] Bill Guinness chasing the Fiats until they cracked up one after the other and then blowing up, as he and everyone else expected, to let Segrave through on the Sunbeam, was something worth seeing.

We combined another test run with the French Grand Prix (which was also the European Grand Prix) in 1924, this time with the experimental prototype $4\frac{1}{4}$-litre six-cylinder car, which we had previously taken to Le Mans, the chassis of

[1] Written before July, 1957.

which we camouflaged with a monstrous Freestone and Webb
Weymann body and an extraordinarily ugly hexagonal radiator, the whole, to the perplexity of the customs, being registered
as 'The Sun'.

This time we had a full load: Witchell, Bertie Moir, a man
from Hoopers the coach-builders called Michaelis, and myself.
It was quite a hilarious outward journey, for we seemed to get
lost frequently and only Michaelis could—and did vociferously
—claim any knowledge of French. '*Quel est la route pour* . . .?'
spoken in an uncommonly deep-voiced English accent, punctuated our journey at frequent intervals, to the accompaniment
of irreverent laughter.

The race at Lyons justified the journey, with Ascari well in
the lead coming in for a final pit stop just before the end, and
then, with his valves burnt out, being unable to start, letting
Campari through on another P2 Alfa Romeo after the Sunbeams had failed.

We were running that $4\frac{1}{4}$ six-cylinder on the new Dunlop
balloon tyres, which made the drive very comfortable on a
pressure of a mere 16 lb., but also very unsafe under an all-up
weight of 2 tons 11 cwt. They were bursting in the most alarming manner every hundred miles or so, and by Lyons we had
got through all our spares and had to telegraph Dunlops to fly
some more out to Tours by Imperial Airways.

It was on the way back from that race, and while we were
running I think on the very last of those balloon covers, that we
caught sight of another car, as unusual as ours, converging on
our Route Nationale and trailing a cloud of dust. It was going
very fast and which of us was going to get to the Y junction
ahead first appeared questionable. The arrival was in fact
simultaneous, with neither of us giving way to the other.

The car I now recognized as a Rolls-Royce, but like no
Rolls I had seen before—until I remembered that the company had produced their prototype Phantom 1 o.h.v. car at
almost the same time as we completed the experimental six-
cylinder. By an extraordinary coincidence we had crossed one

another's tracks on our proving trials at the same moment in the centre of the vast land-mass of France; and in spite of our camouflage we had been identified after a quick suspicious glance by their crew as readily as we had recognized them.

This was not a chance to be missed. I put my foot flat on the floor, and the speedometer needle of the $4\frac{1}{4}$, which had been showing a cruising speed of around 65 m.p.h., leapt up towards the eighties. The Rolls driver took similar measures—and along we went, continuing side by side between the poplars on the deserted road, for mile after mile, neither car giving an inch to the other, up the hills and down the other side.

There was not a half mile an hour between us, and I suppose we should have continued like this all the way to the Channel coast if the cap of one of the Rolls' crew hadn't blown off and gone spinning away into the dust cloud in our wake, obliging them to pull up after a dozen or so miles. I was quite relieved to see them draw back, having had anxious thoughts about those Dunlops.

Back at the works there was an extended post-mortem on the behaviour of the car, and it was at a meeting between Burgess, Bertie Moir and myself that we decided, because the Rolls-Royce would almost certainly be increasing its power in order to claim superiority over us and we were in any case dissatisfied with the power, particularly at the lower end, that we had better keep two steps ahead and increase our capacity to $6\frac{1}{2}$ litres. And that was how the $6\frac{1}{2}$ was born, out of a chance meeting with our closest competitor.

On the eleven and twelve-foot wheel-base of the $6\frac{1}{2}$ it was possible to put anything from a two-seater to a hearse body with complete assurance of comfort and smoothness. The $6\frac{1}{2}$ and the later competition version on the short chassis, the Speed Six, were perhaps the most successful cars we made,[1] and to our great satisfaction both were faster than the Continental Phantom, the big sporting Rolls-Royce.

The cylinder block and the valve gear were the same as the

[1] *See* Appendix III.

3-litre's, but to make it quieter we altered the cam-shaft drive. We also had to do something about the general roughness of the engine, which was very marked on the early production models. We cured this (we were too ashamed to confess at the time but I don't see that it matters now) by setting the engine on very carefully camouflaged rubber mountings. I think the 6½ must have had the first rubber-mounted engine, and it was a very successful makeshift, giving us silence in a car that already had astonishing flexibility and reliability. Only once did we have to touch a 6½ engine during a race.

It was again left to Duff to fly the Bentley flag at Le Mans in 1924, though this time he was given works assistance with greater readiness and we all felt more closely identified with his solo effort, while I went over with Moir and Hillstead to keep an eye on the pit.

That we won that year, taking the race fairly comfortably from an otherwise all-French field of new 4-litre Chenard et Walckers, Bignans and Lorraines, was an excellent thing for us, for the importance of Le Mans was already recognized. But it also had a bad effect on us, causing our previous healthy modesty to give way to over-confidence. This is too easy for words, was our conclusion. And, as we were to discover to our cost, there is nothing so calculated to send you off on the slippery slope of failure as cocksureness in motor racing. There were to be Bentleys at Le Mans next year, in greater strength, but it was to be a long time, and there were to be many changes in the Company and the cars, before we were to take the chequered flag on the Sarthe circuit again.

* * * * *

Amateur wireless was giving me a lot of fun in my few free evenings around this time. My old passion for gadgetry—and a friend called Spottiswoode—led me into the pleasures and perplexities of the wireless set. Spottiswoode had introduced me, back in 1921, to McMichael, from whose shop in Kilburn

I bought the bits and pieces to make my first set. To my astonishment, this worked, and after joining the Wireless Society of London, I was granted the privilege of a licence— and they weren't easy to get in those days. Until the British Broadcasting Company began operations in 1924, there were only the occasional transmissions from Marconis at Chelmsford, and the Eiffel Tower and American time signals to listen to, but though I continued to build my own ever-more-elaborate sets, the magic naturally began to fade as broadcasting became more popular.

9

THE BENTLEY BOYS

BENTLEY MOTORS lived for just twelve years, and I don't think many companies can have built up during such a short period a comparable fund of legend and myth, story and anecdote. The very nature of the firm and its products, which by chance perfectly matched popular taste in the 'twenties, was one reason for this. The Company's activities, particularly in its racing, attracted the public's fancy and added a touch of colour, of vicarious glamour and excitement to drab lives.

I think it all began with the coming of the Bentley Boys. Their arrival and the recognition and growth of their legend cannot be timed from any particular date; the corps grew slowly, shedding some members and gathering new recruits on the way as our racing activity increased. I suppose in all this nebulous band of drivers, whose club-houses were Mayfair and Brooklands and whose 24-hour Annual General Meeting took place at the Circuit du Sarthe, totalled perhaps twenty. But of these a number were very part-time, driving perhaps only once for us; the hard core was made up of only a dozen or so, and most of these were sporting men of independent means. The public liked to imagine them living in expensive Mayfair flats with several mistresses and, of course, several very fast Bentleys, drinking champagne in night clubs, playing the horses and the Stock Exchange, and beating furiously around racing tracks at the week-end. Of at least several of them this was not such an inaccurate picture.

There will be more about the Bentley Boys later, both on

123

and off the track, but they were such a fascinating crowd
that it might be interesting to look at some of them in-
dividually.

I think the first one I ought to mention is 'Benjy', the late
J. Dudley Benjafield, M.D., bacteriologist and later Harley
Street consultant, tough, thick-set, totally bald and wonderful
fun at all times, except perhaps during the hours immediately
before a race. Benjy worried, a useful asset in a racing driver,
and if his pit work sometimes bordered on the ludicrous (I
don't think Benjy ever finally discovered which way the hub
caps should be rotated on a Bentley!) he was a grand driver
who forgot all his worries about his car and how he would
perform once he got going.

I put Benjy first because, apart from Duff, who in any case
drove privately and was in the trade, he was our first outside
driver. It was our 1924 Le Mans victory that brought him to
Hanover Street where he bought first a long-chassis 3 litre on
which he placed a saloon body large enough to kill all performance, and then the red two-seater with the nine-foot
chassis which Clement had raced in 1923. This provided him
with the speed he wanted, and with it he raced with such
energy at Brooklands that we invited him to share the seat of
a 3 litre at Le Mans the following year. After that he drove for
us at Le Mans in 1926, 1927, 1928 and 1929, in the Six-Hour
and Double-Twelve at Brooklands and in a number of other
less important events.

Benjy was one of our steadiest and most reliable drivers and
an equally strong supporter of off-duty fun-and-games.

Birkin, with the enthusiasm that he put into everything,
created his own legend. To many schoolboys the slight figure
of Tim Birkin—Sir H. R. S. Birkin, Bart.—at the wheel,
with silk scarf flying in the wind, represented the ultimate
in courage, excitement and glamour, the Bentley Boy *par
excellence*.

I think Tim's money came from Nottingham lace; anyway
he never had to do much work for it, and from the end of the

war until he died in 1933 he devoted most of his working time
to cars and racing.

We first came in touch with him when he bought a post-war
D.F.P. with the idea of attacking my old B-class records at
Brooklands, and he first drove for us at the Brooklands Six-
Hour race in 1927. Tim's weaknesses were his love of playing
to the gallery and his complete ruthlessness with his cars; I
know of nobody before or since who could tear up a piece of
machinery so swiftly and completely as Tim. During his brief,
terrific duel with Caracciola in the early stages of the 1930 Le
Mans, he threw a tread just after passing the Mercedes on the
grass verge, and then to everyone's horror, instead of coming
in to change the wheel, continued on the canvas without
dropping speed. When he was finally forced to come in he
was down to the rim with the mudguard smashed all over
the place, and shortly afterwards he brought the steaming,
long-suffering 4½ in again, ostensibly to hand over to his co-
driver.

By 1930 two could work on the car, and Chassagne was
leaping over the counter and making for the oil filler with the
can when Tim's characteristic stuttering voice interrupted him.
Standing on the tarmac beside his car, and pointing at the
near red-hot sump, he called out with almost triumphant
resignation: 'Ch-ch-chassagne, don't w-w-waste t-t-time. P-
p-put it in th-th-through that bl-bl-bloody great h-h-hole
there.' It was sound advice, too; the hole the con rod had
made through the crank-case could have taken Bertie Moir's
fist.

I'm afraid that was the sort of treatment Tim's cars had to
put up with. But there's no question that he was a magnificent
driver, absolutely without fear and with an iron determination,
who—while there was anything left of his car—continued to
drive it flat out and with only one end in view.

He lived equally furiously off the track, his fondness for the
dramatic and unexpected having surprising and often excru-
ciatingly funny results. Life was never dull with Tim around, if

only because of the abundance and wide variety of his girl friends.

He wasn't with the regular team for long, one of his many enthusiasms being for the supercharger, which he quite mistakenly thought would make the $4\frac{1}{2}$ a better and faster car. I'll have more to say later about the 'blower' which did us a certain amount of damage, confining myself at this stage to the fact that Tim, under the patronage of the Hon. Dorothy Paget, was by 1929 running a team of much-modified Bentleys in competition with us, which naturally resulted in our seeing less of him.

Tim won twice at Le Mans, once in the Speed Six for us with Barnato in 1929, and again in 1931 in a 2.3 blown Alfa-Romeo, a make of car he did very well with in his last years.

Incidentally, Tim was not killed while racing. Most people believe he died of his burns after a smash in the 1933 Tripoli Grand Prix, but in fact he only just touched his bare arm against the exhaust at the pits during practice—while reaching into the cockpit to retrieve his cigarette-lighter. His arm was still bandaged when he arrived in London six days later, but it was with general septicemia following mosquito-bite poisoning that he picked up in Tripoli (he had contracted malaria in Palestine during the war) that he was admitted to the Countess Carnarvon Nursing Home, where he died on June 22nd. I saw him for the last time at a party he gave at Ciros, at which he turned up late after having his arm dressed, a few days before he died.

Glen Kidston was a born adventurer, rough, tough, sharp, and as fearless as Birkin. I think I was the only person never to receive the rough edge of his tongue, which could certainly be very sharp at times, and we always got on well together. Glen was a traditional naval officer type, quieter than most of the others and very amenable to discipline. Thick-set, with very powerful shoulders, and good looking, his life seemed to consist of one hair-raising incident after another.

Besides driving at Brooklands and elsewhere with great verve on Grand Prix straight-eight Bugattis and Salmsons, he did a lot of flying. He was in one of the early London–Paris airliners when it got lost in a fog. As it began grazing the tree-tops, Glen braced himself for the crash, and in the subsequent fire smashed his way through the fuselage with his fists and was the only survivor.

He had an equally miraculous escape from his submarine, which became caught in the mud of the sea bed, and came to the surface only long after all hope had been given up.

I shall never forget the sight of his Speed Six in the 1929 T.T. straddled across the hedge after one of the longest and most incident-filled skids in the history of motor racing. He got out of that without a scratch too. He drove for us at Le Mans in 1929, put up fastest time in the Irish Grand Prix that year, and won at Le Mans with Barnato in 1930. He had many other drives, including less fortunate ones with the 'blowers', and he was not only fast, but one of the steadiest drivers we had.

Glen's luck finally broke when he was in Africa. He had just taken the London–Cape Town record, and was touring the Union in his little Moth, which was heavily overloaded with unstrapped baggage. Bumpy weather set it loose in the fuse-lage, and the 'plane suddenly broke to pieces in mid-air without giving him a chance to get out.

Jack and Clive Dunfee were the tall, good-looking sons of Colonel Vickers Dunfee, C.B.E., a well-known figure in the City, where he was responsible for the creation of the City of London Police Reserve, and became its commandant. Jack and Clive both had to work for their livings, and I think they found the pace rather fast sometimes. After all, Barnato was spending money at a tremendous rate, and even Tim Birkin, Glen Kidston and Bernard Rubin's scale of spending at that time took some living up to.

The Dunfees had quite enough to buy themselves racing cars, however, and Jack had done some outstanding work at Brooklands and on the Continent in 3-litre straight-eight

Ballots and 2-litre blown Grand Prix Sunbeams before he drove for us; and Clive, a shade quieter and also less experienced than the determined, irrepressible Jack, on an Austro-Daimler and an Alfa-Romeo.

When Clive got married to Jane Baxter he gave up racing, but came back again, very much out of practice, for the 1932 500-mile race at Brooklands, in which he shared a car with his brother. Both his wife and Jack were among the thousands who saw the 8-litre Bentley go over the top of the banking, and kill the driver. That was the last race for Jack, too; and it is on theatre programmes that his name is now so often seen.

S.C.H. 'Sammy' Davis, as Sports Editor of *The Autocar*, was not strictly an amateur, and of course he drove many other makes at this time, but he obviously qualifies as one of the most active Bentley Boys, if only for his and Benjafield's effort with the 3 litre in 1927, when they brought the sole survivor from the White House Corner holocaust home to victory.

Sammy was a figure in the racing business for so long that a meeting at which one did not see him pacing about, sporting his inevitable black beret, asking questions, exchanging jokes, on familiar terms with everyone, was unimaginable. Sammy was celebrated as a somewhat severe pit manager in his own right, and even wrote a book on the subject, which perhaps made it harder for him to accept orders in the Bentley team. However, the records speak for themselves: he drove for us three times at Le Mans, and took second place for us in the 1929 and 1930 Double-Twelves.

George Duller split his loyalty between horses and motor cars; he was equally happy with either so long as they went fast, and if less consistent and more excitable than some, he was a very useful driver to have in the team as he had the happy knack of bringing things back on to a harmonious level at difficult moments with his bright and breezy casual manner and steady refusal to take offence. He shared a ride in the 'black' Le Mans of 1926 with Frank Clement, was second into the 1927 White House tangle, vaulting the hedge from the

A page of bent Bentleys: the 1926 Montlhery car after our abortive attempt on the 24-hour record; a shot I took at dawn after the 1927 Le Mans tangle; and Hayes trying to knock off his wheel in the 1929 T.T.

Above : This is the Le Mans road as we knew it in the early days
Below : Refuelling a 6½-litre at Le Mans, using our new outsize funnel

cockpit of his 3 litre in his best steeplechasing style, and notched up the first 4½'s win with Clement again in the Grand Prix de Paris at Montlhery in 1927. He once partnered Baron d'Er-langer, international banker, international playboy, whose wit and dry humour left an indelible mark in spite of his brief stay with us; the Baron and George together, one sardonically imperturbable and accepting the other's slapstick and practical jokes with a poker face, made an unforgettable pair.

It was Barnato who encouraged us to bring Bernard Rubin, a friend of his, into the team, and together they partnered the winning car at Le Mans in 1928 after the terrific tussle with the Stutz. Rubin was an immensely rich Australian who, like most of the others, was in it *pour le sport* and enjoyed himself with gusto.

Then there was Dick Watney, who drove once for us and had a difficult time sharing the car with Clement, who was about two feet shorter; L. G. Callingham, also a once-only driver; and, of course, dear old 'Chass'. Jean Chassagne had been in the game since goodness knows when; he had certainly been driving fast cars when Edward VII was on the throne. A lifetime as a pro had taught this quiet little grey-haired Frenchman all the tricks, and while there may have been more vivid, faster drivers than he, you would never find him at a loss in any situation and he was as canny as they come. Chass, who had driven for Coatalen against us in the 1922 T.T. and the 1925 Le Mans, would work for anyone, anywhere, any time, and could always be relied upon. Poor Chass; he finished up in the hands of the Nazis, who gave him such a wretched time during the last war that he died.

Frank Clement was, of course, our professional full-time driver; I've mentioned him several times already, and, although he lacked the amateur status of the others, he matched their spirit completely and also drove consistently well, par-ticularly with the 3 and 4½ cars, and with much success and in more races than any of them. The short, squat, mischievous-faced Clement, with his unmatched technical knowledge, was

I

a tremendous asset to the team from that first win at Brooklands in 1921 to the 1930 Le Mans, and he was in the winning car in four major races during this time. His pit work, incidentally, was the least spectacular, the calmest and the fastest. Frank was too methodical ever to get flustered.

Bertie Moir's fund of outrageous and improbable stories, punctuated by demoniac laughter of a unique timbre, were essential ingredients of the Bentley Boys' life blood. After competing in a couple of Georges Boillot Cup races and a Le Mans with us, Bertie was off racing for several years 'for domestic reasons', returning to the cockpit in the 1930 T.T. by bringing a blower 4½ into first place in class. During his 'rest period' Bertie did a lot to help us on the racing side, looking after the pit at Le Mans in 1926 and 1927. He did much towards developing a policy of procedure and technique which made ours the fastest team of its day, and achieving this efficiency by a form of enlightened discipline which surprised people who had seen the light-hearted Bertie only off duty.

And lastly Barnato, the best driver we ever had, and, I consider, the best British driver of his day. I shall have more to say about Woolf Barnato and the leading role he took in Bentley Motors and its downfall. But it is as a driver that we want to consider him now, and to understand him in this role it is necessary to know something about him as a man.

'Babe' Barnato's background was, to say the least, colourful. His grandfather, with the uncompromising name of Isaac Isaacs, was a shopkeeper in the East End of London in the mid-Victorian years. His son Barnett, a dashing, fiery fellow with a driving ambition, assumed the familiar Christian name of Barney, changing his surname to Barnato, and at the age of twenty-one, with nothing more than some slight stage experience and £25 in his pocket, went out to join his brother in Kimberley and make his fortune. In this he was prodigiously successful, buying a claim in the Kimberley Diamond Mine and floating companies with pioneering abandon. After reaching an amalgamation agreement with Cecil Rhodes, which gave them joint control of all the Kimberley diamond mines, he set about digging for gold on the Rand. By the 1890s he was fabulously rich, chairman of the Barnato Consolidated Mining Company, the Barnato Bank, and numerous other concerns. His son, Woolf, was just two years old when he brought him back from Cape Town, and on a calm June night off the African coast Barney disappeared overboard. Suicide was the verdict; but Barney Barnato had no worries to cause him to take his own life, and there were many who benefited from his death.

Babe inherited all his father's canniness and business acumen, and to this he added a love for the spectacular and the dramatic in both his business and private lives. As a sportsman he was a determined, almost dedicated perfectionist, and with his great physical strength, keen eye and razor-sharp reactions he was outstanding at anything he took up. His vitality and restlessness, his complete self-assurance and boyish, appealing appearance, gave him an irresistible charm. It is not surprising that most women threw themselves at him (a thing he always enjoyed) and that he was married three times: in 1915 to the American, Dorothy Maitland, by whom he had two daughters, to Jackie Claridge, the daughter of a Californian coal magnate in 1932, by whom he had two sons, and again a few months before he died in 1948.

Babe was the epitome of the international sportsman-financier-playboy, and no one can have had more fun in living this role. Of Kidston he once wrote:

'He was the *beau ideal* of a sportsman. The word fear had been expunged from his dictionary . . . a resourceful and gallant driver with a flair for any kind of mechanism—a combination of tender hands and a keen judgement plus that indefinable will to win that means so much . . . the most perfect host . . . and a good talker and a better listener. . . . A man about town when in the mood, a man of action in another.'

The words of this obituary of Kidston which appeared in the *Daily Telegraph* in 1931 over Babe's name could have been written for his own seventeen years later.

Having once determined, after careful thought, to take up a sport, he applied himself with religious concentration, starting from the most elementary principles, learning every step by his own experience and disregarding all second-hand advice. He once wagered £500 to £100 that he would reduce his golf handicap from seven to scratch in a year, and of course he was successful. When he took up cricket he was being tried as wicket-keeper for Surrey within months and played for that County several times. He took a fancy for horse breeding in the 1930s, and the Ardenrun Stables were soon producing winners. At a party in Cannes—cruising in the Mediterranean was one of his pleasures—he once wagered that he could beat the Blue Train back to London. Although he liked his drink as well as most of his set and could consume a bottle or two of champagne without any trouble, it wasn't in his nature to make rash bets even when he was drunk, and he would never dream of driving under the influence.

Cold sober, he set off in his 6½ Bentley when the message came through from a friend at the station that the express was drawing out, drove straight through non-stop to Calais, where he took the next boat to Dover and was in his flat four hours before the boat train pulled into Victoria. This was the sort of challenge Babe enjoyed.

His consuming passion in life was to excel, and whether it was in athletics (his physique made him a natural heavy-weight boxer), speed boat or motor racing, he was always successful. 'I think the danger of motor racing is greatly over-rated,' he once wrote. 'It is not as dangerous as it seems.' And he considered life insurance as being 'not worth while'. But he was as shrewd and imaginative in his attitude towards racing as he was towards his business, and took precious few risks. Babe knew very well the sort of racing to avoid, and after weighing up the odds would turn down certain drives, just as he didn't care for track work and avoided the more dangerous events. What made him such an outstanding driver were his keen eye and judgement, his courage, discretion and self-discipline. He was never flustered and never looked as if he was in a hurry. At Mulsanne Corner on the Le Mans circuit it took a stop-watch to prove that he was the fastest driver round, and not the slowest as he appeared to be.

Babe was the only driver in my knowledge who *never* made a mistake, and he always drove to the book, keeping perfect position in the field, and religiously within the permitted revs, following all instructions to the letter. As Chairman of Bentley Motors at a time when I was still in charge of the racing but no longer even managing director, our relations might well have become delicate, and a man of less substantial character than Babe could have made conditions impossible by perhaps attempting to override me, etc. But as a driver he regarded himself as an ordinary member of the team, accepting if need be the second-string car without demur, and suggesting by his manner and his attitude that it was something of a privilege that he had even been included at all.

At the 1928 Le Mans, in which he drove the slowest team car, I had told him to keep station just behind Brisson's Stutz, judging that this would probably rattle the ultra-temperamental Frenchman. For lap after lap he did this, suffering periodic showers of stones when Brisson deliberately wagged his tail, until he was unable to stand these insults any longer and squeezed past the Stutz right in front of the packed stands, offside wheels in the gutter spraying up fountains of water, and with his fingers raised in the appropriate gesture. I joined in the laughter at this, then gave instructions for him to be slowed; but the next time he came round he had automatically resumed his position, satisfied that he had made his point.

This brings us to the matter of discipline in the Bentley team, and I'm going to break off to say a word or two about my relationship with the Bentley Boys.

It was a curious one, being part father-confessor, part

schoolmaster, who was always happy to climb down from the rostrum to join in any classroom foolery. On duty these young men (who were not all that younger than me) accepted my leadership and the racing discipline completely because they accepted the fact that if they didn't it would be the end of their unpaid services, the vacancy being filled promptly by one of the numerous contenders for a place in the team.

Although I had to refuse a lot of invitations because I hadn't the money to return hospitality on their lavish scale—nor the time for that matter—I fitted in well enough at their parties and always enjoyed myself. When they were not yachting in the Mediterranean, ski-ing in Switzerland, shooting in Scotland, or just playing in Cannes or Le Touquet or Paris, the parties were often held in Grosvenor Square, the south-east side of which was known to every London bobby and taxi driver as 'Bentley's Corner'. Here, parked in the square which had no parking problem thirty years ago, were to be seen usually half a dozen or a dozen green $4\frac{1}{2}$, $6\frac{1}{2}$ or 8-litre Bentleys (the limousines for town transport occupied by chauffeurs) outside the adjoining flats of Birkin, Barnato, Rubin and Kidston—*la crème de la crème* of the Bentley Boys. On other nights there were usually informal gatherings at the Grosvenor, the Ritz, Claridges or one of the more intimate new night clubs. When I could afford it I enjoyed these too.

An odd but a happy relationship, in fact; but on the other hand their girl friends could be something of a menace. At races I saw to it that the drivers kept them well under control and well out of sight—which meant out of the pits. Socially it was not so easy, their variety and abundance often being an embarrassment. On three occasions, I remember, I was begged by three different drivers to meet 'the most wonderful woman you've ever met, W.O.', and each time it was the same 'wonderful woman'. We knew each other pretty well by coffee at the end of the third meal.

Chinetti is the only other driver to have won at Le Mans three times; Babe Barnato remains the only driver who has entered the classic three times—three successive times—and won it on each occasion. To have failed at Le Mans would have been an unbearable rebuff, Babe being inclined to take failure as a self-inflicted insult.

It is difficult to say which was his finest drive, for he won many times at Brooklands too; I think honours are probably evenly shared between the 1928 race, which he won after a terrific duel with the Stutz, with cracked frame and dry radiator, and 1930 when he and Kidston battled for $10\frac{1}{2}$ hours against Caracciola and Werner. For eighteen laps, in the early stage, too, when he was constantly passing and being held up on the corners by small cars, Babe's lap time varied by less than 15 secs.

'I don't do any training for a race,' he once said. 'I keep moderately fit, hunting in the winter, cricket and golf in the summer. But of course you oughtn't to have too bright a time just before, not too many parties. . . .' After it was all over, however, it was a different matter. Once he celebrated with one of his outsize parties at which all the waiters were dressed as drivers, complete with helmet and goggles. Another, and perhaps the most lavish and memorable he ever gave, was at Ardenrun, near Lingfield, his vast red-brick mansion in Sussex, which Babe called his country residence, but I thought was more like the Savoy, swarming as it always was with maids and footmen and valets in every corridor. Ardenrun was no place for a quiet week-end, and never knew one during his tenure; its end, like its closing years, was sensational and dramatic, a fire razing it to the ground one night.

I've still got the invitation to that Grand Prix de Danse in June, 1929, to celebrate Barnato's second and Bentley's fourth victory, lavishly decorated with drawings of inebriated Bentley Boys being pursued by Eton-cropped flappers in short-length evening dress. The bars are shown as specially built pits flanking the front drive which is—and was in the event—dangerously alive with fast cars.

Intending 'competitors' had to supply such personal details

as cubic capacity and hobbies, and charabancs were provided
'for the convenience of those competitors or passengers whose
cars are ditched or docked' from Grosvenor Square.

The hours were the usual 10 p.m. to 6 a.m., but the gaiety
had still not faded long past dawn, when the prizes for the
prettiest girls were awarded. A wild drive down the drive in
No. 1 Bentley, 'Driver: Barnato or Birkin-au choix', was first
prize. 'Safety belts and police whistles must be worn' was the
condition of winning the consolation prize—the same ride, with
Benjafield at the wheel.

By such happy means did Barnato manage to get through
eight or nine hundred pounds a week, when the pound was
worth three or four times its value today.

Babe, always a big-car man, began his Brooklands racing
with a vast 8-litre Locomobile he had brought back from
America. He had gone on to score a number of firsts in the
following four years with Talbot, Wolseley, a garish Calthorpe
and a Mercedes, becoming a Bentley customer in 1925, when
he bought a short-chassis 3 litre on which Jarvis fitted a very
pretty two-seater polished aluminium body. With this car, the
prototype of the later 100-m.p.h. catalogue model, Babe won
several major races at Brooklands, and, partnered by Duff,
raised the world 3-litre 24-hour record in September, 1925, to
95.03 m.p.h.

It was at about this time that his seven-year lawsuit over
the famous 'Barnato millions' was settled in his favour—and
the Bentley finances were *in extremis*. Already a convert to our
cars, could he, I wondered, be persuaded to extend his interest
to our finances as other less affluent enthusiasts had done in the
past? He was already sympathetic to our cause and there
appeared to be a good chance that here might be the source of
capital we so desperately needed.

One night I went round to his flat and, over a whiskey and
soda, told him our troubles.

'You know things haven't been easy, Babe,' I began, and
he nodded. He knew a great deal more than I had suspected

about our business side and was soon asking a lot of searching questions about sales, publicity and our future plans.

It is probable, I think, that if I hadn't opened up first he would have come along to me instead.

Anyway, towards the close of 1925 it really began to look possible that the critical years of barrel-scraping, of loans and extended credit and incessant worry, were at an end; that a new and more hopeful era was opening for Bentley Motors under the comforting shelter of 'Barnato's millions'.

10

DISASTERS ACCUMULATE

I THINK it would probably be tedious to say any more about the series of financial crises which came about at the time of the introduction of the six-cylinder 6½-litre car. There wasn't a day without anxiety and when we did not have to confront the dilemma of having a new model which we knew we could sell, and at a substantially higher profit than the 3 litre, but which was so expensive to get out of the experimental and into the production stage that on several occasions I was certain we were going to go under and drown.

But before we go back to Barnato and the second phase of Bentley Motors, I think it is worth mentioning briefly what happened to our cars and those who drove them after that rather breathless moment when John Duff brought his 3 litre first over the line at Le Mans in June 1924. None of our racing was very distinguished—of several events I am thoroughly ashamed; but there was always a certain amount of fun, and we were learning; that was the important thing, we were learning.

Now that we've entered the Le Mans era this seems a good moment to say a few general words about the race as it was in the 'twenties. First of all it was a genuine and very severely regulated production sports-car race for full four-seaters with virtually no permitted modifications to the engine or chassis. Hoods had not only to be carried, but in the early years the cars had to be driven with them up for twenty laps, and ballast equivalent to three passengers had to be carried right through the race. Then not only did all spares and tools have to be carried in the car, but only the driver was allowed to refuel the car and carry out all maintenance and repairs.

Secondly, the road was everywhere so narrow that there was often scarcely room for cars to pass, and had a very rough surface which often used to break up entirely on the corners. No attempt was made to bank or smooth out the corners or clear the verges of obstructions, and of course until 1929 the road went right into the suburbs of Le Mans itself, with a 12-m.p.h. hairpin to negotiate, giving a total lap distance nearly 2½ miles longer than today's.

All this, together with numerous other factors like the quality of fuel and tyres available, has to be borne in mind when comparing the fastest Bentley lap speed at Le Mans of 89.7 m.p.h. with that, some twenty years later after the Second World War, of 96.7 m.p.h. on a billiard-table-smooth road with wide, gently banked corners.

Prompted by our success in a race that had already achieved the stature of the premier sports-car event in the calendar, Louis Coatalen decided to enter a couple of his 3-litre six-cylinder Sunbeams in the 1925 Le Mans; and so for the first time we weren't going to be the only British contenders, and for the first and last time we were to be faced with serious British opposition. The situation, with Segrave, Duller, Davis and Chassagne making up the rival team (three of them later becoming Bentley 'regulars'), matched on our side with equal ebullience by Bertie Moir, Benjy, Frank Clement and John Duff, led to much leg-pulling, although the issue to both sides was an all-important one.

There was practice at dawn that year, and the pits were on the Hunaudieres Straight. There, at an early hour, we would find Segrave, looking even more dour and pessimistic than usual, a perfect target for our coarse humour; and there was always entertainment to be had at Mulsanne, watching him wrestling his way round, his mouth shaping the most dreadful oaths.

That year there was good cause for his depression. Something was seriously amiss with the Sunbeams, and they had had to be sent for attention by Dr. Coatalen in Paris, while the drivers were making do in practice with a standard touring Talbot-Darracq. This car was in the pits, awaiting the arrival of de Hane, and Duller and I were by ourselves in the Hippodrome Café, gazing idly at the car, when George suddenly said, 'Let's give the old boy something to cheer him up, W.O.'

When I asked him what he meant, he simply beckoned to me to follow, and in a very short time had made a neat adjustment to the choke cable so that it was operated by the accelerator pedal.

Segrave turned up a few minutes later, nodded towards us, made a few sour remarks about things in general, started up the makeshift vehicle on which he was supposed to accustom himself to the course, and drove away. When he left us he was trailing only a largish black cloud, but long after he had spluttered out of sight a great smoke screen was ascending above the distant pines towards Mulsanne.

I think it is generally known why we failed that year, giving the race to one of the $3\frac{1}{2}$-litre Lorraines. We had carried out careful fuel consumption tests, but with the hood folded, forgetting that the first twenty laps had to be covered with it raised, the additional air resistance playing havoc with our calculations. On top of this Bertie Moir opened the round with a tremendous tussle with Segrave, the two cars way out in front of the rest of the field, their hoods flapping and billowing in a 100-m.p.h. gale.

Bertie at his most determined is very determined indeed, and I should of course have slowed him down. Instead of which, after only nineteen laps he failed to appear, and was next seen making the long trek back to the pits on foot, leaving behind a perfectly good Bentley with a bone-dry tank.

When Duff was faced with the same predicament a few

laps later, he responded in a less inhibited way towards the refuelling regulations. His approach to the pit was at a run, panting out as he arrived, 'I want some more petrol, W.O.'

'Of course you can't,' I told him brusquely. 'You know it's not allowed.'

'It's my car and I'll do what I damn well like with it,' he replied, grabbing a can and disappearing before I could stop him.

It wasn't for another thirty years that I discovered just what happened after that. The car was surrounded by officials when he got back to it, he told me, and it took a good deal of ingenuity and patience to distract their attention long enough for him to pour petrol into the autovac to take him to the pits, at once resuming work on a perfectly sound petrol pipe line.

Clement took over the car later, working his way up through the field and getting in front of the last surviving Sunbeam, until some forty laps later when he had to retire with carburettor trouble. And that was the end of the first 'black' Le Mans for us.

.   .   .   .   .

Before the next Le Mans came round there was a good deal of Bentley record-breaking activity. In those days, when sheer speed and endurance counted for much more with the public than it does now, even comparatively unspectacular records being rewarded with headlines in the papers, it was sound policy to have a go at records from time to time, quite apart from the valuable experience it gave us. We learnt an awful lot, for instance, from the attack we made on the 'D' class records at Montlhery in the spring of 1926.

The car we took out to France in March was a nine-foot chassis 3 litre, for which Gordon England had provided a very light, beautifully streamlined single-seater body, so simple that it could be taken off or put on again in ten minutes.

We had some merry, but strictly non-professional, excitement in Paris on the way out. The party consisted of Barnato,

Benjy, Frank Clement, George Duller, Bertie Moir and myself—and a friend of Barnato's whom we shall call Brown. Now Babe numbered some gay young men among his friends, but none could match the spirit of Brown, especially in Paris in the spring, in already quite light-hearted company.

After a good dinner at the Carlton Hotel in the Champs Elysées, everyone said they were going out to see the bright lights; Bertie and I were too tired and decided we would go to bed.

During the course of the night they all kept drifting back, singly and in pairs, in various stages of inebriation—all except Brown, who had last been seen making off in the opposite direction to the Champs Elysées with an intent expression on his face. At half past four in morning I was knocked up by the night porter; the British Embassy was on the line, the voice at the other end informing me that a certain Mr. Brown, believed to be of our party, was in debt to the tune of £26 at a house of ill-fame, and would we please go along with the money and bail him out.

Bertie and I, far too cross to feel like Good Samaritans, took a taxi to the address, where we were at first warmly welcomed as new customers, and, after explanations and the payment of the debt, were handed Brown's clothes. Brown, however, was still in far too excitable a state to leave the premises voluntarily, and Bertie and I were finally reduced to frog-marching him down the front steps and into the waiting taxi.

Even that wasn't the end. The night was yet young for Mr. Brown, who hopped out at the first red (traffic) lights. We never caught him, and saw no more of him until the next morning when we bailed him out again—from the Gendarmerie this time.

What we were after at Montlhery was the 24-hour record, which Barnato and Duff had taken the previous September in Duff's own 3-litre Bentley, and above all the 24-hour record at above 100 m.p.h. The prestige to be gained from travelling at 100 m.p.h. for a day and a night in a 3-litre car would be enormous, and at that time, with financial crises raging worse than ever and a horribly blank two-year interval since we had had any sort of competition success, we desperately needed something to shout about.

The luck wasn't with us that year, though, the worst year I think in Bentley Motors' history. The drivers complained that the sorbo-on-aluminium seat was too uncomfortable, and after I tried it out, incidentally having no trouble in putting over 100 miles into the hour, I agreed with them. It wasn't the track surface that caused this discomfort, it was more the shape of the seat. The trouble with the track, though of course it is very much rougher today, was that it was too smooth. At Montlhery we found ourselves during the testing period running at constant revs all the time, and this brought its own curious trouble with universal joints which failed to get lubricated because they never altered their position.

We had our first crack on 31st March, survived for rather over twelve hours, and took a dozen or so records at speeds of around 100 to 104 m.p.h. before the engine burst. A month later, and after a lot more work, we tried again, improved slightly on our previous times, until the engine went again.

This was infuriating. I really had set my heart on the 24 hours at over 100 m.p.h. and I was certain the car was easily capable of it. Nobby Clarke and his men installed another new engine, and we gave this an exhaustive test.

The valves were the cause of the trouble, repeatedly breaking up and falling into the cylinder. We just couldn't understand this, and in the end I got Clarke to put the oscilloscope on to it. This revealed that the valves were fluttering wildly at dead on 3,250 r.p.m. We had, in fact, hit a 'valve spring period', and we couldn't think what to do about it. The simple cure would have been to fit larger tyres, but this was no good either as there was a primary cam-shaft period between 3,150 and 3,250 r.p.m. In the end we fitted smaller tyres and went up to 3,450, which the engine seemed to stand quite happily and which would give us the speed we would need.

Still everything went wrong; even the weather was as nasty as it could be, and after waiting several days for a clearance, it was still looking threatening when Barnato went off just before mid-day. He did the first hour at just over 104 m.p.h., and then it began to rain, the rain turned to hail, a strong wind arose, turned to a gale, and it became dark ages before it should have done.

We huddled in the pit, a frozen, sodden group, while the little streamlined Bentley pounded round and round the steeply banked white concrete circuit for hour after hour. Without headlights, and guided only by marker lanterns, the car with its trailing cloud of spume and spray gave the eerie impression of a piece of mechanism on a huge machine that is under control only by some engineering miracle. It seemed impossible that human hands were guiding it.

In spite of the diabolical conditions Barnato and Clement managed to do the first 1,000 miles at over 100 m.p.h., and there was no question that we had a lot in hand if only the weather would give us a chance.

Early in the morning Barnato came in from his second spell, after succeeding in putting the average up to 101 m.p.h., and I could see that even he was just about all in. So together we went back to the hotel in my car, had a good stiff drink and a wash, and got into some dry clothes. Duller was at the wheel then, and I could hear him easily while I shaved, the engine note fading only slightly as he came down from the banking on the far side of the track.

Suddenly the engine died and at once cut clean out, reminding me momentarily of that night crisis in Coventry when the B.R.1. was on its bench test. I rushed out of the bathroom, downstairs and out into the forecourt to the car. I could hear that the engine had restarted by the time I had jumped in, and I sat there with my finger on the button, holding my breath, waiting.

A few seconds later the engine note expired again, and there was complete silence until I could bear it no longer and

Above : Dudley Froy's record-breaking 4½-litre

Below : First and second in the 1930 Double-Twelve at Brooklands

"MARTELL
for
AGE
and
QUALITY

Daily Express

NO. 9,403.   MONDAY, JUNE 23, 1930.   ONE PENNY.
TO-DAY'S WEATHER: Showery.

DRAMA OF NEW BRITISH SPEED VICTORY

HEROIC STRATEGY WINS GREAT ROAD RACE.

DRIVE OR BURST DECOY TO GERMANS.

SICK MAN'S FEAT.

MILLIONAIRE WINS FOR ENGLAND.

By HAROLD PEMBERTON,
"Daily Express" Motoring Correspondent.

LE MANS (France), Sunday, June 22.

CAPTAIN WOOLF BARNATO, the millionaire British sportsman, and Lieut.-Commander Glen Kidston, driving a Bentley car, to-day won the great twenty-four hours' road race at Le Mans after an Anglo-German motor racing duel that will remain historic.

CAPTAIN H. R. S. BIRKIN.

CAPTAIN BARNATO IN THE WINNING BENTLEY.

AIRPLANE FALLS IN CHANNEL.

THREE MEN FOR TH LIVES

TRAWLER

"Daily Express"

DOVE

BRITAIN'S SPEED RECORDS.

The world's speed records on land, in the air, and on water are held by Great Britain.

In the Air.

Squadron Leader A. H. Orlebar travelled at 357.7 miles per hour.

On Land.

The late Sir Henry Segrave did 231 miles per hour.

British riders and machines have also just won the Light-weight, Junior, and Senior Tourist Trophy races in the Isle of Man.

On Water.

A Leading Article entitled
"MR. BALDWIN AND LORD BEAVERBROOK
—the Truth About the Crisis"
APPEARS ON PAGE TEN.

£800 FOR AMATEUR 'NEWS SNAPS.'

FASCINATING NEW HOLIDAY CONTEST.

These are the sort of headlines we got every year after Le Mans. The other pictures show the last of the old and the first of the new Bentleys: a two-seater 8-litre (*lower*) and the $3\frac{1}{2}$-litre Rolls-Bentley I took on a six weeks' Continental test (*upper*)

drove off flat out for the track. There was still a horrible quietness when I pulled up at the pit, and, even more curious, there was Duller, who should have been driving, running down the track. Of the car there was no sign at all.

Saunders appeared from behind the pit, and together we found it in the end, completely wrecked, upside down in the ditch bordering the road circuit which branched off from the fast banked track at Montlhery. And underneath it, apparently dead, was one of our mechanics, Wally Hassan.

It wasn't till some time later that we could piece together what had happened. Duller, it appeared, had got into a nasty skid at the top of the banking, had gone through 360 degrees several times and had eventually come to rest, with the engine stalled, on the grass. Very shaken, and already tired and sopping wet, he had re-started and driven into the pit and got out, intending to get someone else to take over. But there was no one there; everyone else had, like Barnato and I, gone off for a clean-up and something to eat, leaving Hassan and Saunders to look after things.

Wally today is a very distinguished engineer, with magnificent work behind him at Jaguars and Coventry-Climax, but in those days he was very young, very keen and very ambitious. He had also had very little driving experience, but, seeing Duller arriving looking so groggy and obviously incapable of driving again for a while, he had decided that this was his opportunity to show what he could do and save the day for us at the same time. Before Duller could prevent him, Hassan was in the driving seat, had started up and was away.

You had to be a very good driver to handle that sensitive short-chassis light car on greasy concrete at around the 100 mark, and I think it is to young Hassan's credit that he managed a third of a lap before he got into a long slide, which took him through the barrier on to the road circuit, twice over and over —and into the ditch.

Of course he had done what he had thought was the right thing, but in merely getting into the cockpit he had broken

K

the regulations, and any records after a non-registered driver had taken over would not have been recognized.

Somehow Saunders and I got his limp body into the car, still uncertain whether or not he was alive, and drove off to the nearest doctor's house. He wasn't very helpful, informing us by sign language and Gallic shoulder shrugs that he could do nothing, so, by this time feeling rather desperate, we rang up the American Hospital. 'Bring him along—we'll look after him,' they told us promptly; and we drove the now semi-conscious Hassan as gently as possible into Paris. They kept him for three weeks in a private room, and then refused to take a penny for their services.

I had been determined that the Bentley should be the first car to do a hundred miles for a day and a night, and after we had sorted out all our mechanical problems there had been nothing to stop us—except the awful weather combining with a piece of well-intentioned foolishness. We had failed, and it was a failure I felt more deeply than any other in the Bentley Company's history.

Incidentally, Hassan wasn't the only casualty of that unfortunate affair in France, for I developed congestion of the lungs while we were working on the car. Like most people, I particularly dislike getting ill abroad, where everything is unfamiliar and you don't feel you can trust anyone who doesn't even talk your own language. One morning a sinister-looking nun marched into my room with a black bag, turned me firmly over on to my front and, still in complete silence, stuck a dozen little glass flasks all over my back, filling them with something nasty-smelling and very inflammable, and then setting fire to them.

Bertie Moir, doubtless attracted by my cries for help, came in in the middle of the operation. The expression of horror on his chubby face made me forget the agony, and my laughter set all the little glass flasks a-tinkling like sleigh bells.

Curiously enough this mediaeval witchcraft did the trick all right. The vacuum created when the oxygen was exhausted by the flames in the cups must have drawn out the poison in some mysterious manner, leaving me with a mass of scars but with cleared lungs.

．　　　．　　　．　　　．　　　．　　　．

There are no excuses for failure in motor racing, though we all continue to try to justify ourselves; and it is especially tempting to attempt self-justification to your own board of directors after the expenditure of much time, effort and money. I felt very badly about our Le Mans failure in 1926, which, following the 24-hour record disaster, was a serious blow to the Company, and one which could have been avoided.

Probably our first mistake was to carry out our record attempt at Montlhery so near to the date of the race, spending weeks away from England when I should have been looking after the work at the factory. Not that we went into it in a light-hearted sort of way. Nobby Clarke, who came over with us for the first time this year to supervise the mechanics, did noble work in preparing the three cars, and all of us put in hours of work on minor adjustments, fuel testing and so on in the week before the race, apart from the normal routine practising.

For 1926 we had two strictly works cars, both standard short-chassis 3 litres, to be driven by Sammy Davis, Benjafield, Clement and George Duller, and a 9-foot chassis '100-m.p.h.' 3 litre—the catalogue term being a mere euphemism after Clarke had finished with it. This third entry came about as a result of 'Scrap' Thistlethwayte's dissatisfaction with his OE 30/98 Vauxhall, which he never seemed to be able to make go so fast as Clive Gallop's standard 3 litre. 'Scrap', a handsome, debonair playboy but no mean driver, wanted above all else to drive at Le Mans, but he knew he stood no chance with his 30/98, and Gallop (who had long since left us) invited him to share a Bentley's cockpit.

'All right—but only if it's a 9-foot chassis model,' 'Scrap' told him, and I agreed to our preparing the car 'Scrap' bought and running it from the pits as if it were one of the team on condition he could get a body on to this chassis that would meet the tough Le Mans regulations. Martin Walter of Folkestone eventually managed this after a good many difficulties, and a nice job they made of it.

We were a big party that year, arriving at the Hotel Moderne, where the mechanics always put up, and the Hotel de Paris, which was always our headquarters, by various forms of transport seven or eight days before the race. Clarke turned up at one in the morning, with Captain Head of *The Autocar*, who always helped with the timekeeping, Miller the electrician, and three tons of equipment in a 30-cwt. Ford truck which they had hired in Dieppe. The driver, it appeared, had entered into the competitive spirit rather too strongly, and full throttle for fifty miles played havoc with the heavy load, the nerves of his passengers and the water supply. In the pitch dark, miles from anywhere except a forbidding-looking château, the radiator boiled dry, and they had had to grapple with a massive and very fierce guard dog before they got any water. A second trip had been necessary when the French driver poured the water into a red-hot radiator, and by the time they arrived they were all in a demoralized state.

The French contingent was a strong one, with a pair of sleeve-valve 4-litre Peugeots, three works 3½-litre straight-eight Lorraines and a brace of 3-litre Aries, one of them in the hands of Chassagne, and all of them with experienced drivers like Brisson, Bloch and Mongin. This race, we realized, was going to be no walk-over for us; the opening laps demonstrated that, one of the big Peugeots coming round with a clear lead, which it held until the early hours of the morning when the broken road surface fractured its windscreen bracket. The driver then threw the entire windscreen into the pit, and, amid very Latin excitement a lap or two later, was disqualified. The other Peugeot went out with a flat battery soon after, and we managed to hold our position among the Lorraines without extending ourselves too much.

Duller was the first to go, after breaking the lap record while in the lead, burying himself in the sand at Arnage, digging himself out again, and finally retiring with valve trouble. Soon after dawn the short-chassis car came in with a broken rocker arm. That left us with Benjafield and Davis's car against the three Lorraines, and things became quite exciting during the morning when they managed to get past the third of the French cars while the second was in for a long call at the pits. It seemed obvious an hour or two before the end that we couldn't win, but with Sammy gallantly answering the 'All Out' sign, it seemed possible that we might manage second place.

There were just twenty minutes to go. Sammy had gone past the packed stands, with everyone shouting with excitement, only a few seconds behind the Lorraine, and was visibly gaining. And that was the last we saw of him.

My watch went ticking on, the hands moving past the ten minutes; the Lorraine went by, followed by one or two of the smaller cars; and Bertie Moir and I exchanged agonized glances. I know of no time in motor racing more awful than the moment when your car fails to appear, and it is hard to describe the agony of helplessness you go through while awaiting news. When the situation is as critical as it was in the last stage of that 24-hour race, it can take years off a pit manager's life.

At last, when the race was almost over, and Charles Faroux, the venerable chief of the Automobile Club de l'Ouest, was already making his way on to the track with the furled flag, the news filtered through. Sammy, it appeared, had followed orders and got past the Lorraine, but he had overtaken it very close to Mulsanne, had entered the corner much too fast, and had well and truly cast number 7 into the protective sand barrier. He was digging furiously, it was said, but when the flag fell there were still several hundredweights of sand round the Bentley's axle.

Poor Sammy! It can happen to the best of us, and he was

so overcome with shame that I did my best to conceal my fury. After the previous year's failure, we had needed to win that Le Mans. That none of our cars completed the course was nothing less than a disaster, and I returned to London in an awful state of mixed self-recrimination, anger and depression. We simply couldn't afford to go on like this, wasting time and money and energy which could more profitably be employed in the production of cars to sell. . . . We would have to give up racing entirely; that was it, we would scrap the racing department and concentrate on making some money. Perhaps later?

At the next board meeting I announced this intention, to a new chairman and a new set of faces round the table.

11

BARNATO'S MILLIONS TURN THE TIDE

I'VE said a certain amount about Woolf Barnato the sports-man, the international playboy, the racing driver, and this was the Babe I knew in the early days when he drove Bentleys at Brooklands and helped us a great deal in his record-breaking attempts. I knew at this time that there was another Barnato, the financier son of Barney, who had perpetuated the fortunes of his father and had even added to them through his numerous mysterious and intricately involved interests in the City; but I saw nothing of him before it began to occur to both of us simultaneously that this fabulous wealth and our poverty would require to be compensated in some degree if he was to continue to enjoy himself driving our cars. The moment when this was first discussed that evening in Grosvenor Square and we began to talk together about figures—other figures than revs per minute and miles per hour—this other Barnato emerged: Woolf Barnato, financier. It was a very interesting discovery.

Of course there were clues to the nature of this second Barnato: his single-minded determination, his unusual ability to concentrate, his moral toughness, and his extraordinary parsimony over little things, which made it impossible, for example, for him ever to offer anyone a cigarette. This apparent meanness, in contrast to his lavish hospitality, was a standing joke, and it was the ambition of many of us to get our fingers inside the gold cigarette-case which he always carried in a long, specially tailored pocket in all his suits. One of us—the indomitable Bertie Moir—did succeed and claims to this day to carry the scars from the flange of that gold case across his knuckles. Usually after the day's work the office staff would all gather at the Bristol opposite the new offices in Cork Street and have a few drinks before they went home. But the evenings when there was a round on the Company Chairman were very few.

Perhaps it's an oversimplification and also uncharitable to call this failing meanness. Barnato was very conscious of his wealth, and at a time when there was less social equality and less security, as well as a good deal more poverty than now, I think he was over-anxious not to appear patronizing and to avoid giving the impression that he threw his money about. He never liked lending money, and anyone in debt to him was not allowed to forget the fact. Assets might be several million, his attitude seemed to suggest, but every pound note was sacred.

One of his business associates and friends, who is now a distinguished Air Marshal, was misguided enough to borrow a hundred pounds from him en route from America, funds having run short on the trip. On arriving back at Barnato's Grosvenor Square flat together, his friend, conscious of Barnato's anxiety, at once took out his cheque book. 'Do you mind awfully, Babe, I'm a bit low at the moment?' he said apologetically as he began to write at the desk. 'Can I give you some now and pay you back the rest later?'

Barnato's face was a study in disappointment and distress. 'Well, I don't know . . .' he began uncertainly, and glanced at the figure on the cheque he was being handed. It was £99 19s. 11d.

As a business man Barnato was uncommonly perceptive, quick on the uptake, quick to act and quite ruthless. In whatever he did, in work or play, what he wanted next to success was value for money. It was almost a mania with him, as it is with so many rich men. It has sometimes been said that he came into Bentley Motors only for the fun of the thing, because if he hadn't there would have been no more nice Bentleys for him to race, and that this was a shame when several of us, to whom the firm was everything, were dedicating our lives to it.

But like most things about Barnato, neither his motives nor the course of events were as simple as that. His sporting instincts were fundamental, and one of the things I discovered when I met Barnato the Financier was that he also allowed them to take a strong part in his business dealings. He knew that he was taking a gamble when he put money into the Company, but it was a calculated risk. There was a chance that he would lose on the deal, but there was also a chance that he might come out all square—or even make a lot of money.

In the event he didn't come out of it at all badly, in spite of the misgivings of his advisers. The gamble didn't come off and he received a lot of sympathy when he told people that he lost about £90,000 in Bentley Motors. But against that he got an enormous amount of fun and pleasure from being able to race in the team, becoming as a result one of the most famous drivers of his day, and to be a successful driver meant a great deal to him. He gained the distinction of being associated with the *marque* Bentley in its years of greatest prestige; and he was not entirely above such nourishment to his vanity. He had the choice of any of our cars that took his fancy; and he always ran two 6½s, an open one for the country and for fun and a closed one for town and for splendour, and in 1930 requisitioned a brace of 8 litres (chassis price £1,850 each). Even at the lower rate of income tax that prevailed then, he was able to offset a large proportion of this direct loss in tax remission. 'I know nearly a hundred thousand went down the drain in Bentley Motors,' he told someone after it was all over, 'but on one diamond deal during that time I made a hundred and twenty thousand, so I can't grumble.' It wasn't everyone who saw it like that.

Our personal relations remained friendly throughout, thank goodness. Babe and I rarely discussed business, and I think this was partly because he looked on me as an engineer first, racing manager second, and business man third—a poor third. In any case he conducted his business largely through his ambassadors—his financial advisers. These gentlemen, who devoted themselves to preserving and expanding Barnato's fortune, heartily disapproved of their master's rash venture into the motor-car business, which they viewed with the gravest suspicion and of which they were totally ignorant.

Barnato's terms for participation were announced in May, 1926, and they included the devaluation of the existing £1 shares to a shilling, which meant a nasty knock for many of us. If we weren't quite beggars, however, there wasn't much choice for us but to accept if we were going to stay afloat; and of course the sudden relief from financial desperation after all those years was so wonderful that it took a bit of getting used to.

The broom was forcefully wielded. H.M. and Hillstead and a number of others decided that the new regime was unlikely to suit them, and resigned, and the sales department, beside being shifted to new headquarters, was entirely reconstituted. The showrooms' move to big new premises in Cork Street wasn't approved by everyone, even though we should now have space to show several cars at once. People were used to Bentley Motors being in Hanover Street. Cork Street, sometimes described as 'the street of the dead' by retailers, was not a good place for cars, and it was felt that it was bad policy to house all Barnato's cronies in the offices which they had appropriated for themselves on the floors above.

I was as discreet as I could be about all these changes and all the new faces in the old firm. It wasn't an easy position for me, liking and admiring Barnato as I did, regretting the departure of people I had worked with for so long and knowing at the same time that there was no alternative. Hillstead and H.M. both set up as agents themselves, H.M. taking over the lease on the old Hanover Street showrooms under the name of H. M. Bentley and Partners, the combination of name and locale drawing many of the old customers, and new ones who thought this was still the official Bentley headquarters.

At first my position as managing director was unaffected, but it wasn't long before one of Barnato's senior 'advisers' who had by then become a member of the board himself, invited the Marquis of Casa Maury, who had been a friend of Barnato's for some years, to join the Company and share the managing director's duties with me.

On the face of things, Maury's and my temperaments were likely to clash, causing friction if not fire. Although he was an astute business man, he gave the impression of being a social butterfly, a gay, light-hearted aristocrat with plenty of money of his own, a taste for the arts, a man who 'knew everyone'.

If this appointment was intended—and I am not for a moment imputing such a motive—as a move to bring about my resignation, then it failed, for I viewed Maury's playboy pranks and the fascination he held for women in the same light manner as he treated them himself. Apart from his business talents, Maury was no slouch, throwing himself into anything that came along—motor racing or engineering or the air—with tremendous enthusiasm, and showing an unusual talent for anything he tackled. At Bentley Motors he added a further splash of splendour to our advertisements and catalogues, and his good sense of line in bodywork was shown in his own cars, all of which he designed himself. Maury and I had the same interest in motor racing and the same down-to-earth attitude towards it, and soon discovered that we had much in common. We survived happily as joint managing directors until all patience became exhausted, the bull was taken by the horns, and we were both removed from the chair. In our place, one of Barnato's advisers was appointed.

Bentley Motors at once ceased to be a tight, loyal, if occasionally bickering, family unit. 'Things'll never be the same again,' was the sort of comment one sometimes heard at the works now.

.   .   .   .   .

'The Company has experienced a very great demand for a chassis which will take the heavy and luxurious type of closed body and carry it in silence with a degree of flexibility on top gear, and will prove really fast when it is a question of maintaining a high average speed for long distances. After numerous experiments, a six-cylinder engine of 6,597 c.c. was ultimately decided upon as providing ample reserve of power and the requisite speed. In addition, those special features of the Company's four-cylinder engine which have proved so successful have been incorporated, and the result is a car which needs less attention and is cheaper to maintain than any other large high-powered car in the market today. Those many discriminating motorists who have been led to regard the Bentley as the leader in advanced points of design . . . will not be disappointed.'

That's how we introduced the 80-m.p.h. 6½-litre Bentley, the enlarged version of the experimental 4¼-litre car, in its first catalogue which we issued in 1925, a few weeks before its appearance at Olympia. We had sold quite a few—at the chassis price of £1,450—and had it well established on the market before Barnato's regime; but achieving this only by desperate measures, which included a trip by Bertie Moir and me all round the agents in a Weymann-bodied prototype, asking them to pay a deposit against future orders to be supplied at a special discount.

The response was typical of the support our agents always seemed to give us. The Bentley was a car that needed to be *sold* and not simply handed over in the showrooms after a few worn salesmanship clichés. The sort of people who bought a Bentley often demanded intimate knowledge of the mechanics of the car and several trial runs instead of the usual nip round the town, and this called for the qualities of an engineer as well as a salesman's enthusiasm. We were very fortunate in having many men like this among our agents, particularly in the north of England, whose love for the Bentley was as great as our own.

Yorkshire was always a good Bentley area, and there we were served by the Central Garage at Bradford, run by a canny man called Rose. His sales manager was 'Mac' McCalman, whom we first regarded as an awful pest because nothing seemed good enough for him. Time and again he would bring a car back to us with petty complaints, but I soon saw that there was sense in all his criticisms and that he knew what he was about. 'Mac', the finest car salesman in the country, has the dual attributes of absolute honesty and an unique ability to get on with people. Nobody could touch him at that time in his area of Yorkshire among the rich nobility, industrialists and millowners. They all trusted 'Mac' and would never dream of buying a car from anyone else. Later McCalman became sales manager for Lagondas, and to accompany him round the agents, as I did, with the $2\frac{1}{2}$-litre post war car was a complete education in the art of salesman- ship—which he still practises today with Attwoods of Wolver- hampton.

At Blakes in Liverpool Bertie and I got the same warm reception and promise of co-operation as we had received everywhere else. And there I blotted my copybook by being very rude to an American, though I don't think he realized it at the time.

I am a great admirer of American cars now, but at that time they really were rather terrible, and when the President of the Studebaker Corporation, who had just arrived in a Cunarder, turned up for dinner with us all at the Adelphi, I should have warned myself to lie low if the conversation turned controversial on engineering matters. It did, and having been in that dining-room or the bar of that hotel since 1.45, I was tired and touchy.

'I've heard of your cars,' the American said, turning to me. 'Tell me, Mr. Bentley, in your firm, how does your engineer rate?' And then, giving me no time to reply, he told me that the engineer ought to rate exactly nowhere—he was of 'no account in the automobile organization', just there to take orders from the sales guys. 'That's how we manage things, Mr. Bentley.'

I succeeded in getting some admiration into my voice when I told him, 'From the standard of your product, sir, I can well believe it.' And it went down very well.

Our sales guys had a few things to say from time to time, too, nearly always unexpected things, and very often illogical and contradictory things—although, to do them justice, they were only reflecting that strange and perverse thing, public taste.

'A nice low car, W.O., that's what we need; it's what everyone's asking for—something sleek and graceful.'

Ever accommodating, I would take out pencil and rough out something on the spot. 'Like this, with a really low roof line? About five feet?'

'That's it!' Their enthusiasm was always overwhelming, and I would allow it to run riot for a time while we discussed other details. And then I might put in casually: 'Of course this will mean 4-inch-deep seats and a ground clearance of $3\frac{1}{2}$ inches. All right?'

And then the trouble would start. No, the seats must be deep enough for a gouty dowager, and of course the overseas markets insisted on at least eight inches clearance for rutted tracks . . . and so on.

The $6\frac{1}{2}$ litre, which could easily be started in top gear (for those who hated changing), could cruise at 70 m.p.h. in top (for those who liked travelling fast), could accelerate from 0–50 in 12 sec. (for the sportier drivers), and could do all these things with an astonishing smoothness and silence with any sort of bodywork up to an eight-seater landaulette, was intended to keep the salesmen quiet and to reach an altogether wider public than the 3 litre could ever hope to do.

But by no means did it satisfy all of even our strongest supporters. They would come into the showrooms and say, 'You know, there's nothing quite like a four-cylinder; now if only . . .' Foden, of the famous steam-wagons, was one, God bless him, for his devotion did us a power of good. He was pleased with his $6\frac{1}{2}$ all right. 'It's a very nice car, W.O., very nice . . .' and he hummed and hawed for a while. 'But you know,' he suddenly burst out, 'I do miss that bloody thump.'

It was a case of back to the drawing-board. A new four-cylinder they would have, and it would be a new one and a bigger one, for we had got everything we could hope to get out of the 3 litre. And so work was started, in the summer of 1926, on the 4½, which in substance was the Big Six less a pair of cylinders. And one of the first models was in the Le Mans team the next year.

Yes, of course we had given up racing; it was proving too expensive, taking up too much of our time, and we weren't having any luck. We had finished with competition work entirely—but by November we were hard at work preparing the cars for the following June. It was inevitable with Barnato as Chairman, and I had begun to realize the absolute necessity of wiping off those two humiliating defeats. You can't, having once won a race and then failed twice in succession, just lie low and hope that everyone will forget. They don't.

This time it wasn't simply a case of being a good thing to win. We just had to, and that was that. We built up a really disciplined organization for 1927, rehearsing the drivers in their pit procedure, with the aid of a movie camera, until they could have done the job blindfolded. We arranged the oil filler so that by means of a quick-release cap and a hole cut into the bonnet, which now wouldn't have to be unstrapped and opened, and an overflow drained into a tray and operated by the clutch, we should save about 45 sec. per stop. Refuelling was simplified by the use of a giant funnel into which thirty gallons could be poured and allowed to drain in while other jobs were tackled. The ballast, which was always a headache (you can't imagine how difficult it is to secure inside a car the equivalent weight of three adults for twenty-four jolting hours), we placed as a massive, lead-filled steel bar between the dumb-irons, which incidentally gave us very useful additional structural strength and improved the handling characteristics after a refill when the tail became very heavy.

We made a lot of other modifications to the cars and improvements to our pit procedure. For instance we moved the signals away from the crowded confused area where everybody else's were, down the slight hill towards White House Corner so as to help the drivers to identify them, linking up by telephone, with a duplicate in reserve in case of a breakdown. In the pit we had a timekeeper for every car, each with a stacked reserve of watches, as we had discovered that we easily wore through the normal life-span of a stop-watch in the twenty-four hours. Weeks before the race, Clarke had his mechanics trained like a top-line circus troupe—petrol cans just so on the counter for the driver, everything to hand, everything arranged so that the car could be got away in the absolute minimum of time.

This roughly is how we arranged ourselves in the pit we occupied in 1927 and in succeeding years. Looking at them from the grandstand opposite, from left to right you would see first of all me in the corner, with a watch or two round my neck for checking the separating times (between our cars and any threatening opposition) or simply the lap times of any dangerous-looking car. Here, on my high stool, I could get instant news on all the lap times from the three timekeepers at their tables below me on my left, their stop-watches hooked on to little stands, and their charts, which they would progressively fill with careful pencilled figures as the race proceeded, in front of them.

To the right again you might see the pit manager[1] who acted as my number two and was directly responsible for instructing the drivers and passing information to them during pit stops, and supervised the mechanics. In any remaining unoccupied space would be Maury or perhaps one of the other directors who were interested enough to come over—but no other intruders. We had a very firm rule about that, which had at times to be applied with particular severity to the hordes of

[1] In 1926 and 1927 he was Moir, 1928 Casa Maury, 1929 Clarke himself, and in 1930 Ivermee.

young women who followed the exploits of their favourite drivers around the circuits. What happened at the Hotel de Paris was one thing, during business hours another, highly decorative though they were.

At the right-hand end of the pit, like a market-stall keeper with his scurrying minions, would be Nobby Clarke and the mechanics, seven or eight of them, together with their fuel and oil, their stacked tyres and spares and tools of every description, in the years when it was allowed to supply them during the race. And here, too, you might catch a glimpse of one or two of the drivers off duty, lounging about smoking or refreshing themselves lightly at peaceful moments, dozing a while at night, and leaning over the pit counter anxiously in moments of crisis.

Let's complete this picture while we're about it. It's three in the morning, the first faint glow of dawn is showing over the pines towards the Hunaudieres Straight behind us. The grand-stands opposite are less than half full and resemble the House of Commons at the climax of a nine-hour debate on sewage control. Every few minutes there is the faint sound of a rising exhaust note from White House Corner a mile down the track, followed by the sight of distant white beams from a car's head-lights, searching out the gently rising road ahead.

Slowly, too slowly it seems at first, and then much more quickly, the exhaust roar and those twin tunnels of light increase in intensity, the car bursts in an explosion of sound into the pits-grandstand area, where the brilliant light of the arcs instantly kills the beams. Its passing is instantaneous and causes hardly a stir, its recession into the greyness suddenly undramatic.

In our pit one of the timekeepers looks up from his chart. 'Number four coming up, sir,' he tells me, a routine reminder only, for we are being hard pressed and I have had my watch on him. Neither does Clarke along the pit need the information. Ten minutes ago the fuel churns were lined up in a precise row on the counter, the can of oil and overflow tray, the can of

L

water ready alongside. He is there, leaning over alertly, ready
to examine the car as well as he can from behind the barier, for
the track is forbidden territory to everyone except one driver
at a time.

The sudden tension in the pits finds a response among the
crowds. The word has gone round that an important pit stop
is due; there is a stirring in the stands, and in the enclosure in
front of them a few people who have been asleep on the ground
make their way to the fence behind the safety pit.

This time the Bentley's roar drops an octave or two before
it breaks into the glare of the arcs, rises momentarily once and
then again as third and second are engaged, and the car comes
slap alongside the counter. The pit looks like the railings of a
crowded liner just before she goes down, with no one quite
daring to jump overboard; and the only passenger who's
going to take the plunge is the relief driver, standing beside
Clarke, in overalls, gloves, crash-helmet and goggles, waiting
without a word for the refuelling and servicing to be completed.

The driver is out the second the car stops; he's stiff and
tired, but there's one more job before he can sink back on to
the wicker chair inside with a glass of orange and a cigarette.
The *plombeur* is there beside him with his wire and seals and
pliers, moving quickly about his task, and the driver grabs the
oil can, tips it up and leaves it to drain into the sump while he
stuffs churn after churn of petrol into the funnel he has thrust
into the rear tank. Clarke and his mechanics duck as first the
empty oil can and then the churns in quick succession come
flying past their heads.

Clarke can see that one of the rear tyres is badly worn and
needs changing, and passes the word to Moir who shouts the
instructions to the driver. The *plombeur* is still working on the
last of the seals (no water is needed) when the driver loosens
the hub cap with the copper-headed hammer, spins off the
spare, slips the quick-lift jack under the rear axle and swaps
the wheels around—not hurrying unduly, for we discovered

long ago that precise movements are quicker in the long run. Last of all a quarter turn on the Bentley's sensitive shock-absorbers, a wipe over the lamp glasses and windscreen, and then he leaps up on to the counter as his relief jumps down on to the tarmac and slips into the cockpit. A touch on the starter and . . .

Two minutes forty-eight seconds. Not bad. The lead is down to three minutes, but the rival car will have to come in soon and with any luck its pause will be longer than ours.

.   .   .   .   .

I think quite enough has been written about the 1927 Le Mans and I'm going to say only a few words about it. In any case 1928 was a much closer and more interesting race, for the only serious opposition we had in 1927 was Chassagne's and Laly's 3-litre Aries. The crash at White House, when the new 4½ litre came through fast and hit a French Schneider, being followed into the ditch by both the 3-litre Bentleys and another French car, should have settled our chances in the race—just as today it would have killed all the drivers in their chassisless alloy or plastic shells.

In fact it was probably the luckiest thing that ever happened to us, not because the worst injuries were a few scratches, but because the story of the Benjafield-Davis car's survival, to limp home the winner 18½ hours later, made copy that was splashed across the pages of every newspaper on the Monday morning.

The last thing I want to do is to belittle Sammy's and Benjy's achievement, which was magnificent. When I first caught sight of Number 3 crawling into the pit after a long silent interval of uncertainty and appalling worry, her front wheel buckled, frame bent, and headlamp, wing and running-board smashed, I was certain it was all over; and when I went down to White House nine hours later at dawn and saw the wreckage of the other four cars scattered along each side of the road, it seemed miraculous that our survivor was not only still running, but, after a long stop to tie things up with wire and string, was actually gaining on the leading Aries.

When the Aries came in and stayed for a long time due to starter trouble, we nearly caught up; but Chassagne had the car then, the gap widened, and we all began to lose heart.

It was around 1.30 on Sunday, with two and a half hours to go, when Clarke called to me just after the Aries had gone by, 'Did you hear that noise, W.O.?'

I nodded, guessing what his diagnosis would be. 'I think his cam-shaft drive's going. Better hang out the "Faster" sign'—an unkind suggestion in view of the state of the car.

A few laps later Benjy swept past the hunched figure of Laly peering into the open bonnet, and he was still there next time round.

Headlines, photographs, maps of the course, wildly inaccurate and journalistic reports—they were all there in every newspaper the next day: 'British Bentley Car Crawls out of Mass Wreckage to Win Great Race.' What better could we ask for? Le Mans was suddenly news as a result of that piece of misjudgement at White House; the Press recognized that, and it has remained front-page news ever since.

But it wasn't all on the credit side. If the $4\frac{1}{2}$ had run the full length of the race we should have discovered a slight frame weakness—the only way it could have been located—which, as you'll see, led to embarrassment and anxiety the next year, and might well have caused a far worse disaster than the one which had in effect concealed it.

The Autocar gave us all a huge dinner a few nights later in the private banqueting-room at the Savoy. After Bentley Cocktails, Tortue en Tasse au Sherry, Mignon d'Agneaus, Asperges de Paris and half a dozen other courses washed down with Clicquot 1919, Perrier Jouet 1917 and some exquisite Courvassier 1875, Sir Edward Iliffe rose as the Chairman.

'Gentlemen,' he began, 'I feel that there is somebody missing here this evening who ought to be present . . .' At that the curtains behind him were drawn apart and simultaneously there was an explosion and the air was rent by a familiar exhaust roar as Number 3 Bentley, still bearing the scars and mud of Le Mans, drove in to join us.

.   .   .   .   .

One of these days the Americans are going to win at Le Mans, and it may come as a surprise to a lot of them that they very nearly did so some thirty years ago—in one of the most exciting of them all.

With the exception of Germany (Mercedes weren't going to be tempted into a works entry until two years later) all the major car-manufacturing countries were represented at Le Mans in 1928: Italy with an Itala (Alfa-Romeo waited until we retired from racing) in the hands of World Champion Robert Benoist and Christian Dauvergne, France with Arles, and, what was most surprising, America with a Black Hawk Stutz and a trio of Chryslers, all in the hands of front-rank drivers. The Stutz was particularly formidable with its lower frame and superior cornering to the Bentley, and its 4.8-litre, eight-cylinder engine.

Lagonda were also there with 2-litre cars, and Alvis with their front-wheel-drive Smith-Clarke cars, more evidence that everyone was being forced to recognize that the news value of the race—all traceable back to the White House Corner mêlée —couldn't be ignored.

The 4½, a car which had very few teething troubles, was already well established by October[1] and had comfortably won its first race, the Grand Prix de Paris, two months before— though deprived of its prize money and even the cup because the organizers went bust. We entered a team of three of them, and the pairing of the drivers is worth recording because their performance—as well as their cars—very closely paralleled their temperaments.

Frank Clement and Benjy were our first string, Birkin and

[1] We tried to give ourselves nine clear months for preparation.

'grand old man' Chassagne, then forty-seven, the second, and in the slowest of the cars were Barnato and Rubin; Birkin, Barnato and Rubin all in their first Le Mans. Barnato of course accepted his position without question; maybe he was Company Chairman and a very experienced driver at that, but he didn't know the Sarthe circuit or have any but second-hand knowledge of the subtleties of driving in a 24-hour race.

It was a beautifully sunny June day, and the start, with thirty-three overalled drivers pattering across the tarmac to thirty-three immaculately polished cars at the fall of the flag, was more impressive than ever. Away they went, Birkin thrusting a passage through the jostling field and coming round less than nine minutes later with his nose just ahead of Brisson in the Stutz. Brisson was a very good driver and the Stutz was obviously faster than I had thought it was going to be. The Chryslers were well up, too, and that didn't surprise me so much; I knew they were fast and reliable.

I let the team have their head as I knew the moral effect of these opening laps was important, particularly to the rather more temperamental Continental drivers, with the result that first Brisson, then Tim, then Barnato, Clement and finally Tim again, all broke the lap record. Everyone was having enormous fun and the crowds were loving it.

Chiron in one of the Chryslers was first to go out, and then Tim, who was driving with terrific verve, failed to turn up. The news trickled through by the usual bush telegraph that he had had a puncture at Pontlieu, a minor blow but not a disaster, I thought, even though, to save weight, we weren't carrying jacks that year. The next thing we heard was that he had got going again after having to cut away the cords, and was proceeding—according to plan in this eventuality—on the tyre.

Unfortunately, and not at all according to plan, he accelerated into the seventies, instead of the 'reasonable speed' specified, drove at this pace all along the straight, and miraculously got as far as Arnage before the wheel buckled and sent him half into the ditch. Half an hour later Tim came running up the track, his spotless white overalls creased and covered in oil, and panting so hard that he could hardly cry out for a jack.

I didn't have to tell Chassagne what to do; the little grey-haired figure went trotting off, a jack under each arm, on the three-mile trek back to the car. This episode cost us three hours, and put that car right out of the running.

Our Lagonda friends took the next knock, Samuelson in their first car digging himself into the sand at Mulsanne and Baron d'Erlanger piling the second car into his rear. Half an hour later, with the car's headlamps and bonnet in an unnatural attitude and his own face cut about, he sailed past the pits and continued, with a wonderful expressionless nonchalance and regardless of frantic signals to come in, until the finish: a typical Baron performance.

It was also characteristic of the level-headed Benjy to come straight in when he felt roughness from his engine and a light spray of oil over his legs; there was no pressing-on-regardless about Benjy, and he knew that Frank Clement would be able to trace the trouble at once—which he did, to a broken oil pipe the repair to which put them way back in the field.

So at nightfall things were really critical, with the Stutz in the lead, the remaining Chryslers running sweetly, and everything in the Bentley camp depending on the stocky, relaxed figure of Babe, who had settled down to a steady and, as usual, deceptively slow pace behind the Stutz in the old crashed car from the '27 race. How I blessed his reliability and common sense that year, especially when Clement came in for the last time soon after midnight with a cracked frame!

Our hopes rose again when Barnato handed over to Rubin, after a magnificent stop, at the same time that the Stutz drivers swapped seats, and the Bentley came round on the tail of the American car on the following lap and with a hundred-yard lead on the next. What we didn't know was that the Stutz, with its 8-m.p.g. fuel consumption, had taken on forty-five gallons, and while the $4\frac{1}{2}$ was decidedly tail-heavy on corners with a full tank, the Stutz was positively unmanageable at above three-quarters speed.

What we did know then—which gave me a horrible sensation at the pit of my stomach—was that Clement's cracked frame had been caused by the steady once-per-lap strain it had suffered from a diagonal ridge across the road near White House, which had to be taken flat out for the long climb up to the grandstands. It had not been a freak fault but metal fatigue, and it could surely only be a matter of time before the same thing happened to Babe. I sat on my stool, clicked my watch at every passing of the Stutz—and crossed my fingers. There was nothing to do until daylight.

At dawn we were still running second, some way behind the Stutz again, and as soon as there was enough light I got out my binoculars and focused them on the Bentley every time it went by. The half light was maddening, Babe was doing over a hundred past the pits, and I just couldn't tell for sure.

Up to that time we had never injured a driver (we never did) and it was a heavy responsibility to send Rubin off to chase the Black Hawk Stutz and hold off the Chryslers in a car I knew to be potentially dangerous, and yet it just wasn't sense to order caution at White House; better to retire now than do that. Rubin was ready to take the chance, and in fact drove away, clipped seconds off Brisson's lead and passed the American car while it was in for a refuel.

The last spell was sheer agony. The frame had outlasted the other car's by many hours, but it was bound to go some time; the only uncertainty was when? Babe took over, and the Stutz pit, at last realizing our danger, had hoisted the 'All out' sign to try to upset him. Might as well blow at a battleship! Babe, knowing that our only chance lay in Brisson overdoing things himself, and holding on a mile or two ahead, wasn't to be tempted. This was Babe at his finest—and he got his reward at 2.30 when the Stutz stripped a gear.

Four laps to go—only another 42 miles after more than 23 hours' racing. Surely we were home now. We watched the

Bentley coming up from White House, and it appeared at first to be travelling slower than before; but then that rise was always deceptive.

Babe was doing barely seventy when he went by, and none of us needed the thumbs-down signal he gave us to confirm what we could all scc. It was horribly apparent that the bonnet had slipped back and was now overlapping the dash. It could mean only one thing. The frame had gone, the radiator hose would have been detached, and the water must be pouring out.

How far and how fast could a $4\frac{1}{2}$ Bentley be expected to run in this hot weather without water? And how fast and reliable was a Black Hawk Stutz with a missing gear? There were no slide-rule answers; only prayer was left to us.

Somehow Babe nursed that sick, red-hot, suffering car round, and we heard its less certain roar coming up the rise again for the last time, and the flag came down on one of the closest-fought, most exciting—and for us most harrowing—Le Mans ever.

There is a wonderful photograph of Babe at the end, sitting on the back of the seat beside Rubin, bedecked in flowers and quaffing champagne, looking like a prep-school boy who's just scored the winning try. The transparent pleasure he got from moments like this was in perfect character, and in such extraordinary contrast to the keen business man playing the market.

Equally characteristic was Birkin's performance after the early catastrophe. We mustn't forget him. He and Chassagne worked their way slowly up through the field again, from nineteenth place to just behind the two steady Chryslers, and finally Tim, in a last dramatic gesture, went scorching round the last lap at the all-time record speed of nearly 80 m.p.h. *Finis coronat opus.*

12

THE END

NINETEEN-TWENTY-NINE: the Wall Street Crash, a dramatic drop in the stock market in England, growing unemployment, and the threat of a disastrous slump.

In any trade recession, nothing is more immediately affected than motor cars, and the most susceptible of all are luxury motor cars. Since 1927 things had not been going so badly with us. The works at Cricklewood and the service department at Kingsbury had both been expanded, and the fresh injection of capital had given us much of the new machinery and equipment we had badly needed. The obsolescent 3 litre had been withdrawn from production, the 94-m.p.h. 4½ taking its place for our sportier customers, who also had the choice of the faster short-chassis version of the 6½, with a different radiator, higher compression and twin carburettors—the Speed Six. For luxurious Continental touring or as a refined closed town carriage we provided the 6½ Big Six with a variety of coachwork at around the £2,000 to £2,500 mark; and finally we had the new 8 litre on the stocks, a car intended to compete directly with the Continental Phantom Rolls-Royce and to be marketed at a price a shade above it.

How was this looming financial crisis going to affect us? Already by the autumn the trend was visible. In the first half of the year we had made our first-ever profit, thanks to the 6½, of £28,467, and on the strength of this we had erected a machine shop and new offices at Cricklewood. Now we could think seriously of re-forming Bentley Motors as a public company.

But by the end of the summer the sales decline was evident,

and it was a decline that was well above the average for the season. For several years the volume of cheap, mass-produced cars had been growing, and there were fewer and fewer people prepared to pay the vastly higher prices for a hand-built vehicle. Now, with increasing competition, the catalogue prices of all these cars were being reduced as competition became keener. Obviously there were tough times ahead for us.

To cheer us up we had the best racing year ever. We just didn't seem able to put a foot wrong, and I don't think any British firm has ever had such a high proportion of successes in one year. We started off with Barnato and Benjy leading for the first nine hours of the Brooklands Double-Twelve, a sort of dress rehearsal for Le Mans run over two days in daylight because night driving had long ago been banned at that circuit. It was the Speed Six's first official outing, and nothing too worrying happened to it except that the dynamo drive sheared, and Benjy had to remove the component. He drove off again, after hurling it into the back of the car, but some time later we were told that we had broken the regulations and were disqualified. 'But I hope you'll carry on just the same, W.O.,' I was asked, 'just for the spectacle. The crowds are loving it and we've got to think about tomorrow's gate money.'

I'm afraid the answer was brief and rude. We never seemed to be able to make people understand that we didn't indulge in racing for 'the spectacle', or anything except what we could get out of it indirectly in the way of business; a scarcely sporting attitude, some may think, but to survive racing just had to be related to sales and nothing else.

Actually we didn't do so badly in the Double-Twelve, as Sir Ronald Gunter, a rich young man who was a sort of supernumerary Bentley Boy, and Sammy Davis in a 4½ kept the Bentley flag flying, and came home second after a terrific duel with an Alfa-Romeo, just .0003 behind on the handicap-marking formula.

Le Mans can only be described as a walk-over, with

Bentleys 1—2—3—4, the Barnato-Birkin 6½ leading an impressive procession of the big green cars over the line at touring gait, although earlier we had had again to deal with a determined flock of American Chryslers and Stutzs. I had quite a time trying to hold the speed of the four cars down in the later stages that year, and at one point during the morning Jack Dunfee drew up to a crawl beside the pit and bawled out in exasperation, 'What do you want me to do—get out and push the bloody thing?'

Incidentally, this is a point worth bearing in mind when looking through—and perhaps drawing hasty conclusions from—statistical data on race results. It is too easy to assume that in every race every car has been fully extended. This applies to any race—quite apart from the weather and varying road conditions—and applies particularly to any study of the succeeding race speeds at Le Mans of cars that had refused battle when Bentleys were running there.

Nineteen-twenty-nine was Barnato's peak year, too. A week or so later he romped home first in the B.A.R.C. Six-Hour race at Brooklands in the same car, Clement and Jack Barclay won the Brooklands 500-Miles for us at over 107 m.p.h., and in the handicap Irish Grand Prix we took second to fifth places behind the supercharged Ivanovski Alfa-Romeo, though Kidston's was the fastest car there by 4 m.p.h.

So it went on, until the R.A.C. Ulster Tourist Trophy came round again in September, a race I regarded with caution because the handicap formula was all against our sort of cars. At dinner a few weeks before, Birkin had told me that, regardless of our plans, he was going to enter a 4½ Bentley, one of his first supercharged cars. 'You ought to come along as my mechanic,' joked Tim. 'Do you a world of good.'

To his astonishment I said, 'All right, I will.'

Bertie, on the other side of the table, seemed distressed at the idea. 'But you can't do that. It's much too dangerous. You can't go around sticking your neck out.'

We left it at that for the moment, Tim accepting the

implied thrust at his driving with good humour. Bertie, however, knew that I hadn't put the thing out of my head, and
came up with his trump card a few days later. 'Your life
insurance,' he told me triumphantly. 'It doesn't cover you for
racing—so that's that.'

But it wasn't. I had decided that, apart from the fun, it
would be a good thing to discover just what the mechanics had
to put up with and to show them that I was ready to stick my
neck out too. I paid an additional premium for a covering
clause, and set sail for Belfast with Tim and the others.

The T.T.s in those days, run over a thirteen-mile circuit
just outside the city, were always pretty riotous affairs, with
anything up to sixty cars and a quarter of a million excitable
Trloh uppoctators ranged along the banks and in the most hair-
raising positions on the pavements in the villages. How more
people weren't killed—until the 1936 disaster—I can't imagine,
and why no driver or mechanic was ever killed at Ards, where
everything from giant-blown Mercedes to Austin 7s beat their
way around the narrow roads together for five hours, is a
mystery.

Besides all that, in 1929 there were nasty little rainstorms
which broke out on isolated sections, making the surface as
treacherous as ice. Tyre adhesion, in fact, was a problematical
thing and everyone was skating all over the place—all that is
except Caracciola, who wielded the huge white Mercedes with
incredible skill, and in spite of his formula handicap managed
to beat the Austins and Campari's Alfa home.

So far as I was concerned the whole thing was terrifying to
the last degree, with Tim at his most animated, scorching round
the corners in great slides, flat out the whole time in an effort
to hold the much bigger Mercedes. My morale was not raised
by the sight of a 4½ Bentley upside down at the top of Mill
Hill, with a lot of people trying to push its two tons off Rubin
and his mechanic, and then of Kidston's 6½, which had
already won Le Mans and the Six-Hour for us that year,
settled astride a bank and a ditch.

Thank goodness that by then Tim had decided that Caracciola was beyond the reach of mere mortals, and had eased up a bit. I relaxed, and, considering refreshment was called for, reached down for the pile of oranges I had thrown into the cockpit at the last minute. The pace had been too hot for them, too; in fact I could hardly hold them—and somehow roast oranges didn't appeal.

About five hours later, filthy dirty, very wet and very hot, we drew in, consoled at least by a class win and second place in speed.

After all that fun and excitement, the return to London, to a worsening sales situation and a rapidly gathering crisis, was a sobering business. Barnato had gone to America, on business and in pursuit of a new wife, and it was obvious that his business advisers' attitude towards the firm was hardening and that their only ambition was to get their master out as soon as possible and at the minimum possible loss. I was in for a fight, and I knew my weapons were hopelessly inadequate.

When people ask me (and they are too tactful to do so often) why Bentleys went bust, I usually give three reasons: the slump, the 4-litre car, and the 'blower' $4\frac{1}{2}$s; in proportions of about 70, 20 and 10% respectively.

I'll have a few words to say about the unfortunate 4 litre later. The 'blower', or supercharged, $4\frac{1}{2}$ was the car in which I had done thirty laps of the Ards circuit with Tim. Tim, as you've seen, had a constant urge to do the dramatic thing, a characteristic which I suppose had originally brought him into racing. His gaily vivid, restless personality seemed to be always driving him on to something new and spectacular, and unfortunately our $4\frac{1}{2}$-litre car was one of his targets.

To supercharge a Bentley engine was to pervert its design and corrupt its performance. Every engine we built was conceived with an eye first on reliability, then on smoothness and silence, and lastly on sheer power output. Of course we were after speed and acceleration, but not by any falsely induced means; and I always held that the supercharger applied to the

Bentley engine was, by its nature, a false inducer. When we
wanted higher performance we increased the engine size, from
3 to 4¼ to 6½, and finally to 8 litres, with the intention of always
retaining refinement and reliability.

I disliked the easy short cut provided by the supercharger,
which was against all my engineering principles. But unfortunately for the Company, Tim used his charm and persuasion
to induce first Amherst Villiers to build a special blower for his
4½, next Barnato to give it his blessing, and finally the Hon.
Dorothy Paget to put up the money for a works at Welwyn and
to buy and modify the chassis.

These weren't the only people attracted to the idea
by Tim's reputation and the current fashion for the supercharger. Bertie Moir joined him as racing manager, Clive
Gallop as works manager, and quite a number of our regulars
elected to drive them.

It was, I thought, the worst thing that could happen to us.
They would still be Bentley cars, carrying with them the
spurious glamour associated in the public's mind with the
supercharger, and Tim would see to it that they were well
publicized. They would also lack in their preparation all the
experience we had built up in the racing department under
Clarke over ten years. I feared the worst and looked forward to
their first appearance with anxiety.

On June 29th Tim entered his for the Brooklands Six-Hour
race; it soon retired. At Phoenix Park a fortnight later, the two
'blowers' stayed the course and came in 3rd and 8th, but not
without their troubles. In the T.T., apart from Rubin and
Birkin (and I mentioned a page or two back what happened to
them) the third car retired with engine failure. Tim was also
forced to retire in the 500-Miles race two months later, and in
the J.C.C. Double-Twelve the following May none of the
'blower' team lasted out the course.

This list can become tedious; what really counted was that
the supercharged 4½ never won a race, suffered a never-end-
ing series of mechanical failures, brought the *marque* Bentley

disrepute—and, incidentally, cost Dorothy Paget a large sum before she decided to withdraw her support in October, 1930.

It is a sad story, with a sting in the tail. Because Tim managed to persuade Barnato to allow him to enter a team in the 1930 Le Mans (in which none survived) we were obliged, in order to meet the regulations, to construct no less than fifty of these machines for sale to the public.

    .   .   .   .   .

I think it would be a good thing to add a touch of light to these dark pages by mentioning briefly what else happened to us in that last Le Mans of 1930—besides the performance of the 'blowers'.

The team that year was a good one, lacking only Jack Dunfee, who had done so well in 1929. I wanted Jack to drive with Sammy, but Sammy was so strongly insistent that he should take Jack's younger and much less experienced brother under his wing, that I had to give way in the end, and Jack instead drove with Bertie Moir's 'blowers'. Barnato, of course, came back from America for it, intent on doing the hat trick, and stimulated to a state of terrific determination by the presence there of Rudi Caracciola, surely next to Nuvolari the finest racing driver of the between-wars period, partnered by the veteran, Christian Werner, in a works-prepared $7\frac{1}{2}$-litre supercharged Mercedes-Benz.

I don't think Babe ever enjoyed himself as much as in that Le Mans when, after Tim had got past the Mercedes in the opening laps, then torn off his tyre tread and later blown up his car, the pursuit and harrying of Carach was left in his and Glen Kidston's hands. It was a battle royal, with the pair of them slowly wearing down the Mercedes by making it use its supercharger almost continuously instead of only in the emergencies for which it was intended. There was never more than a minute or two between the two cars, and the lead

Back to Le Mans with the V-12 Lagonda. These pictures show the preparation work at Staines, Lord Selsdon getting away after the first pit stop, and the Dobson - Brackenbury car at the finish after a trouble-free run

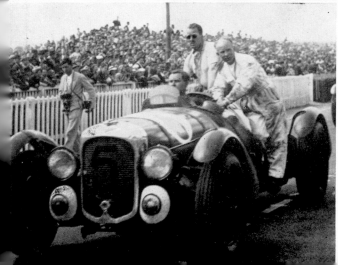

The top pictures were taken at Millbrook House, Colnbrook, where we lived from 1936 to 1945. And this is where we live now, at Shamley Green, near Guildford

changed time and again through the night, until at twenty past three Babe began to draw slightly away. A lap later he was 90 sec. ahead, then 2 min.; progressively his lead increased until he was catching glimpses of Caracciola's tail light down the straight. At 4.20 a.m. the scream of the Mercedes' supercharger died away for the last time, and it came slowly into the pits with dimmed lights. It was all over.

I went round to the Mercedes pit at once to express my sympathy, noticing at the same time that there was water pouring from the car's blown gasket, and had a word with Caracciola. He was very disappointed, of course, but was his usual generous, friendly self. They had not expected to be so hard pressed as they had been, he told me. Their carefully worked-out race forecast, based on our last year's performance, had shown them with a full lap's lead at this stage of the race, confirmation that our policy of not extending our cars unnecessarily paid dividends.

'Never before had I seen such a smile on the face of the "Tiger",' Benjy wrote of me later in *The Bentleys at Le Mans*. But it was nothing to compare with the high-spirited grin of pure glee we all recognized through the oil grime on Babe's face when he came in for his next refill. I slowed his car, and the Clement-Watney 6½, down by 10 m.p.h. after this as there was nothing left in the field to worry us, which again caused some wry cracks among the drivers.

Our retirement from racing after Le Mans was strongly criticized at the time, but I'm sure it was the right thing to do, just as it was wise of Jaguar to withdraw in 1956 at the peak of their success to concentrate their resources on production.

. . . . .

The Olympia Show of 1930 was a sad affair for everyone, and for us it would have been worse if we hadn't had the huge and impressive-looking 8 litre on the stand. That we survived for another nine months is accounted for by the fact that we sold sixty-three of these expensive cars in the period before the

M

liquidation. Kevill-Davies had meanwhile been brought back as sales manager, and had been spending weeks touring the country with a fleet of cars, staging special Bentley Weeks to back up the agents. We did everything possible to keep things going, but it was no good; the brakes were hard on and trade was grinding to a standstill.

I suppose what we should have done was to lay off most of the men (it would have been better for them in the long run anyway) and content ourselves with the erection of a few 8-litre chassis for the occasional overseas order. This is what the liquidator did eight months later, and by doing so succeeded in breaking even.

What we did instead was to design and market a new car, the 4 litre, of unhappy memory. 'We must have something to compete with the small Rolls,' was the Board's verdict. 'A car that will undersell it. It doesn't matter much about the performance, so we'll use the 8-litre chassis—we've got a lot of them hanging around the works. And we don't want any of W.O.'s expensive cylinder heads with four valves per cylinder. Push rods will do.'

I declined as politely as I could to have anything to do with the top half. 'I don't know anything about push rods, I'm afraid,' I said. 'I think you'd better get someone else to look after this cylinder head.'

The 4 litre was in effect a last desperate fling on which most of the firm's remaining resources were spent, but very few were sold because it wasn't a car that could be recognized as a Bentley at all. The Bentley clientele wouldn't have anything to do with push-rod engines, and its performance, particularly its acceleration in top gear, was appalling, the power-to-weight ratio being ridiculous by our standards. If only the huge, heavy 8-litre chassis hadn't been used we should at least have had a car with some pep in it. Instead it was a cumbersome makeshift, with an undoubted long-life expectation, but nothing else that anyone wanted.

.   .   .   .   .

The motor industry nearly always seems to be in a state of boom or depression, and, like a patient with a severe attack of 'flu who thinks he will never be well again, every slump seems like the last. The 1930-1 one was the worst of them all, and while it was on the trade felt that things would never be the same again. Bentley Motors, dependent on its goodwill and on the annual sale of a comparatively small number of luxury cars to the higher-income group, had of course been more strongly affected than any other firm. But we could have pulled through; there's no question of that, and the receiver was already proving it in the five months during which he looked after the firm.

Our continued existence depended on Barnato and his advisers; and, because Barnato and I never afterwards referred to the liquidation, I shall never know for sure just how strongly he was influenced by his financial advisers in his decision to let Bentley Motors go.

By the early summer the writing on the wall was as clear as a Guinness poster, and despair had set in in all departments. And then on 11th July a news item on the City page of *The Times* announced that the London Life Association had applied for the receiver, the sums of £40,000 and £25,000 being due under two mortgages. Captain Woolf Barnato, it stated, was unable to meet these debts. The last item could only be described as a figure of speech; besides, Captain Barnato was in America on an extended visit; he had been there for some time, engrossed in business and personal affairs. The troubles of Bentley Motors must have appeared distant and perhaps rather tedious, and it seems clear that he must have been strongly prejudiced by the reports from London which told him how his losses would be certain to increase unless he allowed the Company to go into liquidation. In America the slump was far more severe than it was in England, and I think the general sense of hopelessness in the business world there must also have had some bearing on his decision.

It was late in June, 1931, when I heard that Barnato wasn't

prepared to put up any more money, and I realized what must inevitably follow. The position was reported to the debenture holders, who decided at once that they would have to appoint a receiver. His name was Patrick Frere, and I only wish he had been our managing director instead of Barnato's crony. He was easy to work with, got on well with everyone, and created an atmosphere of confidence that we had not known for months, by such acts as retaining the design staff in the hope that the tide would turn.

Frere even succeeded in keeping my spirits reasonably high. I had been horribly depressed at first, of course, but it was only a matter of weeks before I heard that a firm of good repute was interested in taking us over, and while things could obviously never be the same as they had been before, I already knew that I should be kept on as chief designer, with a seat on the board.

The firm was D. Napier and Son, Ltd., of Acton, a large and prosperous company which had made some of the finest cars in England up to 1925, but had now concentrated all their resources on aero engines. They were anxious to launch back into the motor trade, and by intending to do so with a luxury car of my design in the middle of such a serious slump, they showed a flattering confidence in our design department. By the end of July, when the negotiations with Napiers were officially announced, I was given leave by the liquidators to start work on this new car.

Their last car had been an overhead cam-shaft six-cylinder machine, of excellent design, great weight and indifferent performance. The car we worked on during those months—the Napier-Bentley—was to be a completely re-designed 8 litre in its general engineering principles, with an engine scaled down to 110 × 110 mm. and a capacity of $6\frac{1}{4}$ litres, like the last Napier. The 8-litre Bentley had had a vibration period which we had only cured with a damper, and so for this $6\frac{1}{4}$ we worked on a new and much stiffer crank-shaft to eliminate this, and a shorter piston stroke. We also planned a modified cam-shaft drive to take up less space and produce a shorter engine.

The Napier-Bentley was, in fact, to be an altogether more lithe and responsive car than the 8-litre Bentley, with a dropped frame to make it lower and lighter all round. It is interesting to speculate how it would have turned out; certainly it would have out-performed the bigger car.

I was feeling reasonably happy about our future plans— which also included a possible new aero engine—when the time came in November for the receiver to apply to the court for approval of the Napier contract. Terms had been agreed, everything seemed to be tied up, and this was to be nothing more than a formality. Frere had even treated the staff to a farewell dinner and theatre. Instead that day turned out to be the most disastrous in my life.

The court was in session, everything was running according to schedule, Napiers' representative had made known to the judge their price, when a figure rose and said, 'I am empowered by the British Central Equitable Trust to offer so much for the assets and goodwill of this Company'; a figure that was, by an extraordinary coincidence, a fraction more than that offered by Napiers.

There was a brief and horrible pause, and then Napiers' representative got up and asked for a brief adjournment to allow him time to consult his principals. This the judge granted, and shortly after the court heard Napiers' new and higher bid.

The other barrister was about to raise his price too when the judge informed the court that he was not an auctioneer and that there would be another adjournment until 4.30 in the afternoon when sealed final bids were to be handed in by the two opposing barristers.

I don't know by how much precisely Napier were outbidded, but the margin was very small, a matter of a few hundred pounds. All I knew that evening was that the deal would not be going through after all.

The confirmation of this bitter news was in the papers the next morning.

'Bentley Motors—Purchase Surprise' ran the headlines. 'The expected absorption of Bentley Motors Ltd. by D. Napier and Son Ltd., the aero-engine makers, will not take place. An unexpected and last-minute bid yesterday afternoon secured the Bentley assets for a rival buyer, a syndicate known as the "British Central Equitable Trust". Nothing is known of the syndicate's intentions. Nor is any director of the Trust apparently identified with motor-manufacturing interests. It is therefore presumed that this financial corporation is acting on behalf of some firm as yet unknown.'

Days passed without news, during which I was in a state of acute anxiety. It was an odd and unpleasant sort of situation not to know who now controlled my future, and the firm which bore my name. I waited for an official word, but none came, and Napier could tell me nothing.

And then one evening my wife came back from a cocktail party at which she had overheard a man saying something which she understood to mean that his company had recently taken over the old Bentley firm. Later in the party she managed to find out the man's name from her hostess.

'It was Arthur Sidgreaves,' my wife told me. 'Who is he?'

'He's the managing director of Rolls-Royce,' I told her.

13

THE 'COMMERCIAL MAN' BREAKS OUT

NAPIER couldn't have been nicer and did their best to cheer me up, confirming that of course I could still work for them, and that, in effect, I should only be transferring my offices from Cricklewood to Acton. When Rolls-Royce, however, decided they had other ideas about my future, Napier's goodwill towards me was put to practical test.

My service agreement with Bentley Motors, Rolls-Royce informed me, was still in force. I was not a free man to select my own future. I was, they made clear, part of the assets which they had purchased, together with all my office furniture, my medals and cups and trophies.

Napier replied, rallying nobly to my defence, by disputing this contention, and actually went so far as to take legal proceedings on my behalf. So there I was, back in court again, with the issue this time a strictly personal one. The judge ended the hearing with the announcement that, as it was presented, he could not give judgement in the case, and advised Napier to re-present it in different form.

By then Napier had already spent a lot of money on me, for the legal expenses alone had been considerable, and so, with the greatest reluctance, they told me they simply couldn't pursue things any further. I replied that I understood perfectly, and we parted on the best of terms.

I am deliberately hurrying through these winter months of 1931-2, sketching in the barest outline, and I think that's the best way. Even now I find it distasteful and depressing to think about them, though I try to do so as charitably as I can. I suppose the nadir was reached when I was instructed in a letter to sell my old 8 litre. I left it with Jack Barclay and walked home, without a car for the first time for goodness knows how many years, wondering if I should ever have another, and wondering, too, just how long I could expect the hundred pounds or so I had left to last.

For several weeks I lived in a sort of vacuum of uncertainty and worry, avoiding meeting anyone I knew, and trying to keep fit by walking round and round Hyde Park. On top of everything else at that time, my marriage wasn't working out. I had re-married seven years before, but unfortunately we weren't temperamentally very well matched, and I'm afraid I may have been too dedicated to my motor cars. Anyway, we were divorced soon after Bentley Motors was sold up.

It seemed inconceivable that Rolls-Royce should want to employ me. What could they do with me? They had their own design staff, and it seemed to me that I would be as embarrassing as a prisoner of war after the armistice signing. I simply couldn't imagine what they might have in mind when I was asked to call at their London head office for an interview with Sir Henry Royce.

It might be called an exploratory interview, I suppose, and I have often wondered what was its purpose. The opening was not propitious.

'I believe you're a commercial man, Mr. Bentley?'

'Well, not really,' I said. 'Primarily, I suppose I'm more a technical specialist.'

'You're not an engineer, then, are you?' Royce asked in some surprise.

I didn't know quite how to answer this without appearing vain. And then I remembered from thirty years back. 'Yes, I suppose you could call me that. I think you were a boy in the G.N. running-sheds at Peterborough a bit before I was a premium apprentice at Doncaster.'

This was accepted with a nod, and I heard no more on the subject. Instead I was offered a job, on not ungenerous terms, a rather nebulous sort of job in their London showrooms as an understudy to Percy Northey who had, like nearly everyone at Rolls-Royce, been there since the company began. Northey, who had years ago brought a Rolls-Royce into second place in the first Tourist Trophy race, looked after the technical liaison with the works, and was due for retirement soon. I was to help him, to attend the morning sales conferences at ten o'clock when any technical points and criticisms were discussed, and ensure that the demonstration cars were in good order.

Whether or not I could have refused is a nice point, and one that didn't arise.

·   ·   ·   ·   ·

Rolls-Royce had acquired, apart from me and my name, the Cork Street showrooms, the works and offices at Crickle-wood, the service station at Kingsbury, and a few 8-litre chassis. The showrooms and works were sold; the service station returned to Van den Plas, from whom we had rented it; the sad survivors of an extinct motor car were shipped to Derby; I had been safely placed out of harm's way; and now— for not only had they paid a large sum for it but to let it die would reflect badly on them—they must justify their acquisition of the *marque*. In fact, the Bentley car must be reborn.

What sort of car was it to be? And was the person whose name it was to carry going to have any say in its design? The second question never arose, for I was not consulted in any way on either the $3\frac{1}{2}$ or $4\frac{1}{4}$-litre Rolls-Bentleys and only asked to comment on the design. The first remained problematical for a time.

When the clouds of the depression had been seen on the horizon from Derby, work had begun on a small $2\frac{3}{4}$-litre bread-and-butter economy car, a sort of scaled-down 20–25 h.p., and intended to be sold at a considerably lower price. It turned out eventually to be as complicated and refined a piece of machinery as its bigger brother, and as the only saving was

in the weight of metal involved, the term 'economy' was a
misnomer, and the prototype was put aside. Actually it was a
very nice little car, carrying a rather dainty radiator on the
same classic pattern as all R.-R. radiators, with a good turn of
speed, as I discovered when I tested it at Brooklands.

It may have been my favourable report on this car that led
Derby to try supercharging it, swapping the R.-R. radiator for
a slightly modified version of our old 8-litre design. This was
not a success. The engine didn't care for the increased stresses
and kept blowing its gasket. So the only supercharged Rolls-
Royce car engine never got off the bench, and the design staff
looked about for other ideas.

Once again Hives came to the rescue, as he had so often
done before and was to again in the future, notably in the case
of the Merlin aero engine, which would never have been
perfected in time for the Battle of Britain without his inspira-
tion. I already had a very high regard for Hives' ability at
experimental and development work, which was by far the
strongest side of Rolls-Royce, and the way he set about the
Rolls-Bentley, and later while I was there the twelve-cylinder
Phantom III, confirmed my opinion.

Hives arranged for work to be put in hand to increase the
power of the new 25–30 Rolls-Royce engine, the successor to
the 20–25, by fitting twin carburettors and raising the compression, and then putting it in the frame of the discarded
2¾ litre. The result was a very nice motor car.

The 3½ Rolls-Bentley was an excellent car on the road,
light and easy to handle, with surprisingly good performance
allied to quietness. Later on it was spoilt, just as the 3-litre
Bentley of a decade earlier had been spoilt, by customers who
put on heavy, unsuitable bodywork, which inevitably, as before,
led to complaints of lack of performance. So up went the
capacity to 4¼ litres, and the same story began again.

The model was launched with the customary R.-R.
publicity—discreet, tasteful and most effective—in time for the
1933 Show, and at the Royal Hotel, Ascot, there assembled by

invitation all the motoring correspondents worthy of the name for a luncheon and trial run. There were three cars for demonstration use, and on these Cox, the sales manager, Percy Northey and I were to take the gentlemen of the Press in turn round a triangular course. Naturally, the purpose was to impress, and it was thought advisable to post scouts around the circuit to ensure that the roads were clear.

It was a very good luncheon, and the three of us enjoyed our afternoon hugely. But the peak of the day for me came when I identified the proprietor of the hotel as the man who had once written a book called *An Innkeeper's Diary*. I had been amused to read in this that one of his guests at his previous hotel had been W. O. Bentley, 'a timid little man'. I invited him to come round with me in the front seat on the last lap of the day, when the brakes were feeling a little tired. By then my eye was well in and I felt I knew the road and the car thoroughly. I had him holding on like grim death before I skidded to a halt in front of his hotel again, and told him who I was.

.   ·   ·   ·   ·

After eighteen months or so with Rolls-Royce, and on the retirement of Percy Northey, I was appointed to a position that was little less indeterminate but which carried the title Technical Adviser to the Managing Director. I continued to look after the demonstration cars, both those attached to the London showrooms, which were, ironically, now situated below the offices in which the original Bentley 3-litre engine had been designed, as well as those belonging to the London agents.

This job was taken very seriously by the firm, and the cars were brought in turn by a chauffeur to my Addison Road house where I was now living, married to my present wife. There I tried them out, first sitting in all the seats in turn while I was driven round, usually taking over myself for a while and driving us both back to the office, where I would submit a report. The Continental Phantoms I would take down to

Brooklands to see that their performance was up to scratch. It was also my business to test other cars, mostly high-performance cars which could be regarded as competitors to the Rolls-Bentley, and this I enjoyed immensely.

I was also expected to take both Rolls and Bentleys over to the Continent for long test runs, just as I had done in the old days with our own cars. The first of these was with one of the 3½s, which I thrashed over the Italian and French passes and ran at high speed along the Routes Nationales for six weeks, the only sure way to discover hidden faults. Another time I took a Continental Phantom II Rolls-Royce on a similar trip and sent in a long report with a number of suggestions for improvements. For instance, on the Continental I got stuck on a corner 9,000 feet up on the Galibier Pass with the petrol boiling away merrily, and as a result the works moved the pipe lines clear of the engine and the pump to a cooler position along the chassis.

Not all these reports and suggestions were received kindly or acted upon. There was, as you can imagine, a certain suspicion of recommendations from an 'outside' engineer by the regular staff of the experimental department and the works, which was increased rather than reduced by being filtered through the managing director. As soon as I got wind of this attitude I made arrangements for direct liaison with Derby, and started making weekly visits to the works, getting to know the men there personally. To leave the dreariness of the London offices behind and head for Derby was like a tonic, and my days there were the happiest and most interesting of my time at Rolls-Royce. Not only did I succeed in damping down the quite understandable distrust they had for me at first, but I made many good friends, some of whom left to join me later and are still my friends today.

There was enormous talent at Derby, so much that it sometimes became congested, which led to frustration among some of the younger technical men. The standards of workmanship and attention to detail were extraordinarily high, and if (rather to my satisfaction) I occasionally found them making the same sort of mistakes that we had made at Bentley Motors, there was never the least suggestion of complacency.

I suppose I should have been grateful for a job that was well paid and which kept me in touch with all the good motor cars of the time, and I certainly couldn't complain of being overworked. But of course it was all rather tame and uninspiring after the exciting and adventurous days of Bentley Motors, and I could never quite throw off the feeling that I was nothing more than a hostage—a dangerous ex-enemy confined (with all reasonable comforts) to my Elba.

By 1934, Barnato, who had bought a substantial number of Rolls-Royce shares shortly before the liquidation, was on the new Bentley board. I saw him often; we were still good friends, if there was a trace of reserve in a relationship which was now on an entirely social level. Business was never discussed between us, and when we talked about the old days it was of our cars and our racing. It was never suggested, by Barnato or anyone else, at any time that I should become a director of Bentley Motors (1931) Ltd.

By an extraordinary piece of mismanagement we had never registered the name Bentley as a trade mark, a fact which the legal men at Rolls-Royce jumped on at once, and one of the first things I had been asked to do when I joined the company was to sign a document authorizing them to apply for one in my name. In addition, and in consideration of my release from paying them a certain sum of money owing at the time of the take-over, I signed a contract which, in the event of my leaving them, debarred me from lending my name to the design of any car or aero engine for a period of ten years.

It was perfectly understood between us that as soon as my service contract expired I was free to leave the company. On my past record, this was indeed considered probable as soon as a likely job came along. I suppose, after all, that I could be considered a car designer rather than a car tester, and I was still only forty-seven.

Just the same, I was undecided whether I should leave the security of this huge company and cast myself into the mêlée again. Finally it was the persuasion of my wife and friends, who knew how frustrated I felt, that made me take the plunge. Though I've paid for it dearly, not for one moment since then have I regretted the decision.

·   ·   ·   ·   ·

In June, 1935, an odd and totally unexpected thing happened. A 4½-litre Lagonda, driven by Hindmarsh and Fontes, won at Le Mans. It wasn't a very spectacular win and the speed was considerably below that of Barnato's Bentley for the first twelve hours in 1930, before he was slowed down. But it was a win and would mean a tremendous fillip for the firm which, like us, had recently gone into liquidation.

On the Friday before the race, I had had to be with Arthur Sidgreaves for most of the day. It was an occasion of some delicacy for me, for my contract had just expired and he obviously expected me to give my decision on the new five-year contract, on better terms than the first, which had already been drawn up. Over lunch we discussed this and that and I awaited the leading question.

Instead, he told me that Rolls-Royce were thinking of making a bid for Lagondas, a subject which was as delicate as my contract, for I had just heard from Dick Watney, who had recently left Rootes, that a friend of his was also about to buy the firm, and that he wanted me to look after the design side. I remained firmly noncommittal on the matter, contenting myself with asking Sidgreaves why on earth Rolls-Royce should think of doing such a thing.

Twenty-four hours later that 4½ Lagonda set off with fifty-seven other cars round the Sarthe circuit, and on the Sunday evening the unexpected news came through that it had won. Dick Watney heard from me first thing on Monday morning. 'Yes,' I told him, 'I'll come if the sale goes through.'

Thank goodness, Rolls-Royce were beaten to it this time by Watney's friend, Alan Good. Good was a Lincoln's Inn solicitor who had decided to break out of the legal rut into the uncertainties of sports-car manufacturing; and now I was back in it again—with him.

14

V 12

LAGONDA is the name of a small town in America, the home town of a Wilbur Gunn, who emigrated to England sixty years ago and began building motor-launch, motor-cycle and three-wheeler engines, and then small utility cars. By 1935, when I went there as technical director, they had acquired through their 2-litre, 3 and finally 4½-litre cars a solid reputation for quite high-performance sporting machines. Somehow the company had staggered through the worst years of the depression, but had never really found its feet again, and when Alan Good took it over, the factory and offices at Staines were in a dreadful state. I was horrified when I went down to see them for the first time; it seemed impossible that a car that had won Le Mans had emerged from such a dilapidated wreckage, and I was thankful that responsibility neither for rebuilding and extending the works, nor the finances, were mine.

At the same time I was rather dismayed to find, contrary to what I had been told, that Dick Watney was to be the managing director instead of Alan Good. Watney, a likeable man, was not in my opinion a big-enough character to handle the responsibility, even with Good as Chairman over him. However, what mattered to me was that I was to be quite unfettered in the one field I knew something about, a change after the diversions and anxieties of Bentley Motors, the frustrations and politics of Rolls-Royce, and I felt quite light-headed with the sense of freedom.

At first, until the new buildings were completed, working conditions in the drawing-office verged on the ludicrous. It was

an ancient tumbledown shed; the rain rattled on the corrugated
iron, and spiders and water fell freely about us. I had known
austere working conditions at Bentley Motors, but nothing
quite like this.

As a first obvious step before we could get our own car on
to the drawing-boards, we decided to re-vamp the 4½-litre
model for which the works was already tooled up. It was a
fundamentally sound if rather coarse basis on which to start, a
six-cylinder, o.h.v. push-rod engine, sturdy, powerful, and with
a quite outrageous crank-shaft roar. It seemed a long step—and
a retrograde one—from the 8 litre and the dainty, involved and
highly refined 3½-litre Rolls-Bentley. But we managed to get an
agreeable high-performance car ready for the Show that
autumn, with rubber-insulated engine mounting and suspension modifications providing greater smoothness and quietness, improvements to the combustion chambers giving about
140 b.h.p. at 4,000 r.p.m. (providing around 95 m.p.h. in top),
and a host of other alterations such as the provision of synchro-
mesh gears and a right hand gear change. It was a good buy at
around the four-figure mark, and later we put the engine into
the V 12 chassis. In this form it remained in production until
the war.

My period at Rolls-Royce had driven home once again to
me the value of time for development: time, that luxury that
only the most solidly founded firms can afford. The big Rolls-
Royce Phantom III car, for example, was begun in May, 1932,
with no less than sixteen designers. Two years were spent on the
completion of the main design, and the first experimental car
was running in June, 1934. But it was another sixteen months
before the car was even announced, and production didn't
begin until May, 1936—four years in all. That was how Rolls-
Royce achieved standards of perfection against which other
companies, without their reserves of capital, couldn't compete.

We had produced the 3-litre Bentley in just twelve months.
At Lagondas we were given rather over eighteen months to
have a car ready for the Motor Show. 'When a renowned

N

designer and his assistants—in this case W. O. Bentley and his technical staff—set themselves the task of evolving a car which shall rank in the very forefront of machines,' wrote one of the motoring journals of the new V 12 Lagonda, 'it would only be a matter of surprise if that car failed to be outstanding.' To us it was a matter of surprise that we got the car out at all. No reasonably conscientious workman likes being rushed; and yet the yearly balance sheets made the impatience of Alan Good and his backers—and also the salesmen—inevitable. We did our best, and I think the V 12 Lagonda of 1937 could have been the best car for which I have been responsible; but I would have given my right arm to have had another two years to develop the car before it was placed on the market.

The V 12 was a very short-stroke engine, with twelve cylinders set in two rows in the form of a 'V'. The short stroke resulted, as we had intended, in great smoothness and flexibility, and no car that I have ever driven has given such an impression of quiet effortlessness. The first road test spoke of the passengers dozing in the back seat at 100 m.p.h.; this was quite practicable, too, for the 4/5-seater body carried very comfortable seats. The performance at the top end was satisfactory and the top speed was well over the 100 mark, but at the lower end there was plenty of scope for improvement, and the 0–50 acceleration time was only just under 10 sec. That, together with points of detail in the chassis design and the steering, were things we would have put right if the war had not intervened.

Soon after production began we put on a show at Brooklands for publicity and general Lagonda prestige. Lord Howe and Stan Ivermee took a V 12 and a 4½ litre down to the track to see how far they could go in the hour. Both were completely standard production models and both had our own saloon coachwork. Brooklands, as anyone will tell you who drove there in 1938, was in a very bad state, and the V 12 damaged a tyre half-way through the run, and Lord Howe had to stop, jack up and put on the spare. In spite of this he managed 101½ miles in the sixty minutes, with a lap at over 108 m.p.h., while Ivermee did just under 96 miles in the same time.

This was good for business, but we had never thought of this big, refined sports carriage in terms of racing at all, and it therefore came as a nasty shock when Alan Good suddenly told me early in 1939 that he had decided we ought to run a team at Le Mans in June.

'But we're nothing like ready for that sort of thing,' I told him. 'If you really want to race the V 12 you must give us at least another eighteen months for preparation.'

Good was adamant. 'If it could be done with the old 4½ then there's no reason why we can't win with this. It's a much better car, and it's a much faster car.'

I'll concede he was right to want the prestige that a Le Mans win would bring the model, but to be left with less than six months to get the cars ready was patently absurd.

'All right,' I agreed after more argument. 'But let's be quite clear—and tell everyone else—that we're not out for a win this time. We're running for what we'll learn from the race.'

In fact we decided to run the cars at a set speed, regardless of what happened to the rest of the field, a mile an hour faster than the 1938 winner's, and see how things worked out. What really counted was what we found when we pulled the cars to pieces afterwards.

We nearly killed ourselves getting the cars ready in time. Stan Ivermee looked after the work, with Kemish, Sopp, Taylor, and one or two others, all from the old Bentley days. I suppose there was some sleep and food for them, but whenever I went down there they were always at it. The most fundamental modifications were the fitting of four carburettors and a much larger petrol tank, and the raising of the compression. But it was all the little bits and pieces (too technical to go into here) that took the time, as they always do in preparation work—so much time, in fact, that we could only try out one of the cars for an hour or so at Brooklands. The other had its first run down to Newhaven to catch the boat.

They looked very low and sleek, and formidable, too, we thought, with their special two-seater bodywork. Arthur Dobson and Charlie Brackenbury were to handle one of them; the other, with his coat of arms emblazoned on the dark green cellulose, belonged to Lord Selsdon, and he and Lord Waleran ('The Peerless Peers') were to drive it under our control.

It was quite like the old days to be going in good company with a team to Le Mans again, and what made it even more pleasant was the welcome I received from everyone, from the customs officials at Dieppe to the scrutineers, and wonderful old Faroux himself, whom I had first met sixteen years earlier at the first Le Mans ever.

I got a shock when I saw the circuit for the first time again for nine years. From the speeds—the lap record had gone up to 96 m.p.h. against Tim's 89 m.p.h.—I should have guessed that there had been some radical changes to the corners and to the road. But I hadn't realized we were going to have this billiard-table surface, with every bend eased, the trees cleared to improve visibility, the road widened everywhere. This was more like track racing. The regulations showed that the whole conception of the race had altered. Now there were no hoods or screens, two-seaters were *de rigueur*, and it wasn't necessary to carry that great burden of ballast that had always been such a headache. Pit work was revolutionized by the use of gravity-fed petrol pumps and other aids, and mechanics were now allowed to work on the cars. You can see what this meant by comparing the time of 27 minutes that the winning Bentley in 1930 spent in the pits, when our pit work was really streamlined, and the 12 minutes the Selsdon-Waleran car was in the pits in 1939. The 15 minutes saved at 80-odd m.p.h. represented twenty miles in the race, or about 2½ laps.

After the 1—2—3—4 Bentley win in 1929, Charles Faroux had written, 'The moment has arrived when the French automobile industry must decide whether to reassert itself or allow the decline to continue.' Ten years later it had reasserted itself all right; there was no question of a few small blue cars tussling five hundred miles behind for the Index of Performance handicap prize. In 1939, besides Wimille's and Veyron's streamlined 3.3-litre supercharged Bugatti, there were big Talbots, Delages and a whole flock of very fast Delahayes, all in the hands of well-known drivers.

The Saturday was blazing hot, with the banners floating in the sun and, as always, what appeared to be half the population of France there, gaily dressed for their great annual fête. And they certainly got their money's worth. The start particularly was as wild as I have ever seen it, the Sommer-Bira saloon Alfa, Louis Gerard's Delage, Chinetti's Darracq and the big Bugatti all fighting it out just as if it was a half-hour sprint run.

With Stan Ivermee handling the pit with his usual efficiency and my wife looking after the only slightly less important downside side, it was as pleasant a race as we could have hoped for, with the two green Lagondas running faultlessly and with only one unpremeditated call when Dobson's exhaust worked loose. They kept scrupulously to their stipulated 83 m.p.h., and slowly, as the French cars tore themselves to pieces, we found ourselves automatically working up through the field from tenth or twelfth place, until the following afternoon when, at four o'clock as the flag fell, there were only the Bugatti and Gerard's Delage (by then fit only for the wrecker) left ahead of us.

That was my last Le Mans, and I've never been back to the Sarthe circuit since. But it wasn't quite my last race. The Outer Circuit August Handicap was one of the few occasions when Ebblewhite, the famous handicapper, was thoroughly caught on the hop. He wildly underestimated the speed that the two Lagondas—the Le Mans cars without wings—could lap at, and Brackenbury and Selsdon were having to cut out at the fork so as not to embarrass him too much. Even so they were miles ahead of anything else, lapping under these conditions at 128 m.p.h.

A week or two later my wife and I were staying on

holiday at the San Christophe Hotel near Miramar in the South of France. The sea was of the incredible shade of blue that only the Mediterranean can assume, the food and wine were beyond compare, that blessed sun blazed in a clear sky day after day—and the hellish doings of Adolf Hitler seemed a million miles away. But, dutifully and reluctantly, I drove the Lagonda up to the top of the hills behind Miramar one evening and switched on the radio. The six o'clock news came through, loud and clear and horribly depressing. Germany was poised to invade Poland; an ultimatum had been sent by Britain. Slowly we drove down the steep road back to our hotel.

The Riviera had already emptied and we were almost the only English people left in the town. By the time we had reached Dieppe, after being almost reduced to pushing the car for lack of petrol, the ominously threatening atmosphere had changed to one of wild disorder. Hundreds of cars were stranded all over the docks and the town, and I got a hollow laugh for pointing out that we had booked shipping space. In the end we sailed without the car like everyone else, and that drab port, Newhaven, looked drearier than ever as we steamed in for the last time on the packed boat.

．　　　．　　　．　　　．　　　．

At the end of 1936 my wife and I had moved from our London home in Addison Road to a house with a thatched roof and a beautiful garden in Colnbrook. From Millbrook House to Staines took only a quarter of an hour, and after eighteen months of driving from London to the Lagonda works I had had enough of it. The west London industrial fringe is not generally considered prepossessing, and it is true that there are some pretty terrible areas of scattered factories and bungalows spread out over a dead flat landscape. Colnbrook escaped all this, and, relieved of heavy traffic by the bypass, has remained an unspoilt oasis in that steel-and-concrete desert. Millbrook was the happiest house I have lived in, and I think we should have stayed there longer if London Airport hadn't come and sat down outside our back door.

Any mild excitement in the Second World War seemed to happen at Millbrook rather than Lagondas. The factory was so craftily camouflaged that it never got a bomb splinter, even from the squadron that blasted Vickers at Brooklands which passed right overhead. But our house was neatly pin-pointed for enemy bomb sights by those famous barrage balloons Jessie I and Jessie II (Jessie I upped and away in a gale one night), and I sometimes suspected that these two plump girls, who were a part of the barrage for Hawker's factory, carried the painted message for Luftwaffe pilots that the factory where I worked turned out thousands of anti-aircraft rockets every day. But bomb stories were boring enough at the time so let's not get involved in them now.

The period 1939 45 was mostly drudgery, as I suppose it was for nearly everybody: a good deal of hard work, long hours and not much fun, though things were made gayer for us by the nearby 956 Balloon Squadron, whose officers often came in for dinner and parties at Christmas and for tennis parties in the summer. Millbrook was never empty or quiet, especially as we nearly always had a nomadic population of W.A.A.F. billettees, and my wife was perpetually busy with her W.V.S. work.

When at last I began to feel that my work at the factory and the night A.R.P. duties weren't really enough, I went to see my old C.O. of 4 Squadron from the R.N.A.S. days, who was now something important at the Admiralty, to ask if I could be of any use in the aero-engine line, but nothing came of that, and I went back to the aircraft parts, the bits and pieces for tanks and the even more unpleasant things like flame-throwers that we were turning out at Staines.

Towards the end of the war, with all the new machinery we had installed and the vast expansion in the size of the factory, it was quite clear that if we went back to cars we could do some quite big things. There seemed, in fact, nothing to prevent us from becoming a major producer in the motor-car market, and when it was obvious that the tide had turned, I began to think about our post-war car.

Alan Good wanted the V 12 back into production, and there was nothing I should have liked better. It would have been a very good car with all the development work we could have put into it. But, apart from the fact that all the jigs and dies had been scrapped, I wasn't at all sure that it was the car the post-war world was going to need. Obviously there were not going to be so many people with money for a luxury machine as there had been, and the cost of motoring was going to be higher. Now that we had all the facilities for quantity production, it did seem unwise deliberately to take the risk with an expensive car, with its acute susceptibility to every trading recession.

In the end we decided on a medium-sized car aimed at the quality rather than the luxury market, a car designed for as high a performance as silence, comfort and a 2½-litre engine would permit. The prototype was very like the current Lagonda, with a body we built ourselves, and performance was quite good, with a maximum around the 90-m.p.h. mark; and with independent suspension on all wheels, the handling was very pleasant. I didn't think we should have any trouble selling this at a competitive price, just above that of the Rover, thanks to the quotation we got from Briggs for making the bodies and frames. And 'The New 2½-Litre Lagonda-Bentley' would be the first entirely new post-1939 designed car. So far so good. Now we had to announce and sell it.

The first advertisements duly appeared, and the first response was a prompt and very firm demand, backed by threat of legal action, from Rolls-Royce that we must withdraw my name at once from the car because it was an infringement of their trade mark. We had an immediate extraordinary board meeting at Lagondas, to which I brought my fourteen-year-old agreement. This was studied with care again, and then I said: 'Let me go up to see Hives and talk this over with him before we get mixed up with litigation. He's not an unreasonable man and I know him well.' Good and the others agreed, and I went off right away to see him at the Grosvenor where he was staying.

Lord Hives had now succeeded Sidgreaves as managing director, which made things easier. I think I've already made clear my admiration for Lord Hives, both as an engineer and as a man. If ever there was a testing time for our friendship, this was it.

In his suite I pulled out the contract and showed him the clause. 'There's nothing in here prohibiting me from using my name on a car,' I pointed out. 'It says that for ten years from 1932 I can't, except, and in smaller print, as the designer. And I've always presumed that after ten years it's permissible, otherwise there would be no point in having a time limit.'

'I agree with you,' said Hives after he had read through the document. 'That's how I would have read it too. I haven't seen this contract before.'

'Well, what about this case you threaten to bring, then?'

But, of course, as he pointed out, a trade mark was a trade mark, regardless of any private contract of this nature. At the same time he thought that it was hard on me and agreed to my suggestion that a new agreement should be drawn up prohibiting me, for a consideration, from lending my name to any motor car for life.

Hives, after agreeing to this in principle and stating the sum they were prepared to pay, said he would confirm it in writing. But unfortunately, although it was really a matter between Rolls-Royce and me, Alan Good said he wouldn't have anything to do with it on these terms and announced his intention to go and see Hives and argue it out himself. I knew what the result of that would be. By strict legal definition I was entitled to nothing, and in any case Good's aggressive manner would be certain to get Hives' back up. Within a few weeks we were neck-deep in litigation.

Lagondas never had a leg to stand on, and when it was my

turn to go into the box—dragged there very reluctantly I might add—I couldn't see how to present my evidence other than in favour of Rolls-Royce rather than Lagonda. The case cost Lagondas £10,000 and the use of my name on the car, and me the substantial sum of money agreed to by Hives, beside the agony of standing witness. There is no place I hate more than the inside of a British court when I am involved, and I have been in them much too often for my liking.

Catalogues were scrapped, advertisements altered, and now it was to be simply, 'The New 2½-Litre Lagonda—designed under the supervision of W. O. Bentley.' That was blow number one to the post-war car. The second was much more serious, the death-blow in fact so far as this company was concerned. We were then, in the mid-'forties, back to the old supply and manufacturing conditions that had prevailed when we had launched the original 3 litre. There was a shortage of everything—plant, raw materials and labour. But this time, under the Labour Government, everything was tightly controlled, and steel more severely than anything else. When we applied for some for the car we were horrified to receive an allocation for just a hundred bodies.

This is absurd, we said; we can't tool up for production on this basis, and anyway what happens when we use that up? What sort of guarantee can you give us for the future? The Ministry of Supply refused us any guarantee, and Briggs, with too much other work to bother themselves with such uncertainties as this, declined to handle the bodies at all. So there we were, with a stack of orders to keep us busy for years, a beautifully equipped works, a new car—and nothing to build it with.

Some years before, the ownership of Lagondas had been taken over by a large finance house in the City who were not directly interested in the car business, although they were very satisfied to leave the firm in the hands of J. R. Greenwood (who had now succeeded Alan Good as Chairman after disagreements) and the rest of us at Staines so long as prospects were promising. Obviously they were not after this crippling blow.

There was nothing else for it, and with all regret, but very sensibly I think, Lagondas was put up for sale; and I was told to put the finishing touches to my own gravestone. I suppose there was no one better equipped than I to try to sell the design of the car for which I had been responsible, and I did the job with as much grace as I could, and with genuine enthusiasm.

I took the prototype down to Oxford and showed it to Sir Miles Thomas and Alec Issigonis after Lord Nuffield had expressed interest in it. But it wasn't really proletarian enough for them. My next call was at Jaguars at Coventry. They liked it too, but as it had a good deal in common with their own cars and would meet the same market, they didn't see how it could be fitted into their programme.

I think it must have been some time in the summer of 1947 when I met David Brown at London Airport and drove him in the prototype to the works. And this, of course, brings us to recent history. The deal went through, the David Brown organization took over the half dozen prototypes and the engine design, which in ever increasingly developed form has since powered their D.B. Aston Martins; while our Lagonda chassis with the same unit was similarly developed and is marketed today, with increased bore and handsome Tickford coachwork, as the 3 litre.

Naturally I was sorry to see the car go, though relations throughout the deal remained very cordial, and when you consider the number of designers and engineers—particularly in the motor business—whose products are only a memory and an entry in an index, then I suppose I am lucky to be able to follow today the progress of cars that were once no more than a few tentative lines on our drawing-boards.

This pleasure isn't confined only to Aston Martin and Lagonda cars. The Bentley cult seems to be as strong today as it ever was, judging by the number you see on the road and the events that are run for them by the Bentley Drivers Club. This energetic body had begun operations some five years after

the decease of the old Company under the initiative of G. K.
Pelmore, Forrest Lycett, the Hon. G. W. Bennet and a dozen
or more enthusiasts for the *marque*; and on 24th May, 1936,
there was a get-together tea at the Old Bell Hotel in Hurley at
which twenty-seven 3, 4½, 6 and 8-litre cars and about forty
founder-members were present. Speed events at Brooklands,
hill-climbs and trials followed, at which it was unthinkable to
turn up in a car that was not in *concours d'elegance* condition;
and teas, film-showings, cocktail parties and dinner-dances
have added a pleasantly gay social touch to this unique and
ever-growing body.

Today it is at its strongest, with Stanley Sedgwick as
President, Colonel Darrel Berthon as Secretary, and a host of
voluntary supporters who have helped to make the club as
influential as it is today. There is a membership now of
around 1,300, an impressive monthly magazine, and a
calendar packed full enough to keep the strongest Bentley-
phile contented.

Unfortunately my own position with the club was rather
difficult at first when I was with Lagondas, but for the past ten
years or more I have kept in close touch, always attended the
annual dinner and a number of the events, and have been
honoured with the position of Patron. It is always a great
satisfaction to see how beautifully the cars are kept and in what
excellent hands they are spending their old age.

Cars have been my business for nearly fifty years now; they
have filled most of my life, given me enormous pleasure and
satisfaction—and worry and heartbreak. Four times—in 1914,
1931, 1939 and 1946—I have been pipped just when things
looked promising; for the world of high-performance quality
cars is an especially tough one, and I should think it is going
to be even tougher in the future. But, given the energy and
ambition I had in 1919, in the context of 1957, I think I should
have another go. . . .

Instead, my only remaining ambition is to continue to live
modestly in this Surrey cottage, retaining an active mind that

allows me to do my consulting work for British and American firms—and a bank balance out of the red. Otherwise an occasional glimpse of the Mediterranean sun, my garden and my hobbies, and above all the companionship and comfort of a very happy marriage keep me contented.

And I have my friends. If the motor industry is a rugged one, the loyalties run deep, and I have many close friends from the days when it was a tight, compact little world, from the roaring, exciting and anxious 'twenties, and the post-Bentley era.

A short time ago we had a party. On the village green outside our cottage seventy or eighty cars assembled, and most of them were green Bentleys—3 litre, $4\frac{1}{2}$, $6\frac{1}{2}$ and the occasional 8 litre. And most of them nearly thirty years old. An the English summer was up to its usual tricks and we couldn't use the garden as we had planned, our low-ceilinged rooms were packed to bursting and the air was thick with smoke, with technical talk, racing talk and straight reminiscence. Besides Bertie Moir, who handled the beer barrel with his usual aplomb, there were many others from the Bentley, R.-R. and Lagonda days; and some 150 members of the Bentley Drivers Club I had never met before.

My wife and I had reconciled ourselves to some inevitable breakages and a mess to clear up afterwards. But everyone was meticulously careful as well as charming, no one drank too much, and afterwards the rooms looked as if they had just been spring-cleaned; we couldn't even find a glass stain or a shred of cigarette ash.

As the last booming Bentley exhaust note faded away that night and one or two of us settled down to some late-hour talk about the old days, I felt that it had all been worth while.

APPENDIX I

'The Bentley Boys': A Racing Record

These figures cover the period 1922–1931 and include only the following races: Le Mans (marked by an asterisk), the Brooklands Six-Hour, Double-Twelve and 500-Miles races, the Dublin Grand Prix, and the Paris Grand Prix. Nor are the supercharged team's results included.

JACK HARCLAY .... Started in one race
                             1st once

WOOLF BARNATO ... ... Started in eight races
                             1st five times (three at Le Mans)

J. D. BENJAFIELD ... ... Started in eight races
                             1st once*
                             3rd once*

W. O. BENTLEY ... ... Started in one race
                             4th once

SIR H. R. S. BIRKIN, BT. Started in seven races
                             1st once*
                             3rd twice
                             4th once

JEAN CHASSAGNE ... ... Started in one race
                             4th once*

F. C. CLEMENT ... ... Started in fourteen races
                             1st four times (one at Le Mans)
                             2nd once*
                             3rd once
                             4th once*

H. W. COOK ... ... Started in two races
                             3rd once

S. C. H. DAVIS ... ... Started in five races
                             1st once*
                             2nd twice

J. F. DUFF	Started in three races
	1st once*
	4th once*
GEORGE DULLER	Started in three races
	1st once
JACK DUNFEE	Started in three races
	1st twice
	2nd once*
CLIVE DUNFEE	Started in three races
	2nd once
BARON D'ERLANGER ...	Started in two races
	3rd once*
R. C. GALLOP	Started in one race
SIR RONALD GUNTER ...	Started in one race
	2nd once
EARL HOWE	Started in one race
GLEN KIDSTON	Started in four races
	1st once*
	2nd twice
H. KENSINGTON MOIR ...	Started in one race
BERNARD RUBIN	Started in three races
	1st once*
R. G. WATNEY	Started in one race
	2nd once*

APPENDIX II

Production Figures of Bentley Cars

	Yearly total	Year	Total
3 LITRE	145	1922	
	204	1923	
	403	1924	
	395	1925	
	295	1926	
	140	1927	
	45	1928	
	0	1929	
	4	after 1931	
			1,639
4 LITRE	50	1931	
			50
4½ LITRE	273	1928	
	260	1929	
	138	1930	
	56	1931	
	6	after 1931	
			733
6½ LITRE	58	1926	
	127	1927	
	99	1928	
	129	1929	
	126	1930	
			539
8 LITRE	100	1931	
			100
		Grand total ...	3,061

Of the 3-litre cars 506 were 'Speed Models' and 15 '100-m.p.h.' models.

Of the 4½-litre cars 54 were supercharged.

Of the 6½-litre cars 171 were short-chassis 'Speed Sixes'.

APPENDIX III

The 6½-Litre Bentley

RACING RECORD IN MAJOR RACES

Le Mans Grand Prix d'Endurance ...   Entered twice, won twice, second once.

Brooklands Double-Twelve ...   ...   Entered twice, won once, second once.

Brooklands 500-Miles   ...   ...   Entered twice, won once, second once.

Brooklands Six-Hours   ...   ...   Entered once, won once.

Irish Grand Prix   ...   .   Entered once, second once.

Tourist Trophy   ...   .   Entered once (crashed).

RACING RECORD OF LB 2332 ('OLD NUMBER 1')

1929 ...	Le Mans ...	...	1st
	Six-Hours ...	...	1st
	Irish G.P. ...	...	2nd (1st in speed)
	Tourist Trophy	...	Crashed.
	500-Miles ...	...	2nd (1st in speed)
1930 ...	Le Mans ...	...	1st
	500-Miles ...	...	1st

(This car, fitted with an 8-litre engine, was destroyed when it went over the banking at Brooklands in the 1932 500-Miles race.)

A report on the 6½-litre car compiled by the Bentley Drivers' Club, under the guidance of its President,

Stanley Sedgwick. It was first published in *Motor Sport* in February, 1949, and is here reproduced in abridged form by courtesy of the Editor:

As early as 1925 it became apparent to the designer of the by then world-famous 3 litre, that an entirely different type of car was required, to meet the needs of a different class of motorist. Such a car should have the attributes of a high-speed touring chassis, should be capable of carrying the enclosed coachwork of the time, and should handle like a dignified town-carriage. The development of such a car was no mean task and W.O., ably assisted by his designing staff, set about designing a prototype based on their experience with the 3 litre. The six-cylinder evolved closely followed the well-tried layout of the 3 litre, but incorporated several new features.

The specification of the first production models was as follows:

Engine ... Six-cylinder, 100 mm. bore by 140 mm. stroke, 6,597 c.c.
Four overhead valves per cylinder.
Coupling-rod-driven overhead camshaft.
Compression ratio 4·4 : 1
Duralumin rockers, ball-end tappet screws.
Dual ignition by two magnetos.
Thermostatically controlled water circulation.
Celeron reduction gears, 30 by 60T.
Autovac fuel feed. Single Smith type 50 BVS/C carburettor.

Clutch ... Single-plate type, Halo-lined. Single-plate clutch-stop.

Gearbox ... B.S. type. Indirect ratios: 3rd, 1·278; 2nd, 1·823; 1st and reverse, 3·364.

Steering ... Worm and sector type.

Rear axle ... Spiral bevel gears, ratio 4·16 to 1.

General ... Wheelbase 11' and 12'. 33" by 6·75" tyres: 21" rims. 19 gallon petrol tank. 'Telegauge' petrol gauge. Smith double-pole lighting and starting. Road speed at 3,500 r.p.m.: 84 m.p.h. Chassis price: £1,450.

The first models had a half-engine-speed dynamo, driven from the camshaft and located on the aluminium bulkhead as in the

3 litre, but the majority of these chassis were later modified to the engine-speed dynamo driven from the nose of the crankshaft, the radiator shell being altered to suit. Few, if any, of the original radiator shells are in existence today.

At this point it is convenient to deal with some aspects of the operation of that somewhat complicated, but nevertheless reliable type of camshaft drive, the coupling-rod crank-drive—frequently referred to incorrectly as the 'eccentric drive'.

Broadly the system consists of a helical gear-driven, three-throw crankshaft, having the crank throws at 120 degrees, to which are coupled three specially designed connecting-rods, which in turn are connected to a driven crankshaft of similar dimensions direct coupled to the overhead camshaft. The upper big-end bearings of these connecting-rods are fitted with an expansion-compensating device to counteract changes in crankpin centres due to temperature variations, and it is this device at the camshaft end of the coupling rods which appears so complicated to the uninitiated.

Another development introduced with the advent of the $6\frac{1}{2}$ litre was the ball-ended tappet screw, designed to give 100% valve-tip contact with the tapper-adjuster screw, despite the use of overhead rockers, thus eliminating the centre-punch effect of the orthodox tappet-screw on the valve stem face, and, by so doing, reducing the need for tappet adjustment to very infrequent intervals.

Another refinement used for the first time as standard equipment was the crankshaft torsional damper of the conventional multi-disc type. Fitted to the front end of the crankshaft, this self-contained unit, when adjusted to slip at 60 to 80 foot-lbs., required attention only at infrequent intervals.

A thermostatically controlled circuit of unconventional design completed the layout of this very efficient power unit. It consisted of two distinct water circulation circuits regulated by a thermostatically controlled valve of ample proportions. In the 'cold engine' circuit the thermostat by-passed the radiator except for a small leakage to prevent freezing-up. With the engine hot, the valve in the open position allowed the coolant access to the radiator. The whole system of cylinder block circuits was concealed within the cylinder block and the front cylinder block jacket-plate.

The single Smith 5-jet Type 50 BVS/C carburettor supplied the mixture to a water-jacketed induction pipe of the 'Ram's Horn' balanced-flow type.

A starting device or strangler and a mixture control is incorporated in the design and consists of a cam-operated sleeve sliding over the well jet which, in the full-rich position, closes the air supply to the well jet, and in the full-weak position opens a series of holes in the base of the port block.

The steering-box, of the orthodox semi-reversible worm and segment type, was of entirely new design incorporating a meshing arrangement consisting of an eccentrically machined, slotted-valve bearing for the segment shaft. After removing the securing tab and slackening off the sleeve pinch-bolt, the rotation of this sleeve moved the segment into or out of mesh, according to the direction of rotation. End flat was adjusted by the method common to all Bentley chassis, viz. the steel valve with inclined slots secured by two pinch-bolts at the base of the box casting.

As in the 3 litre, the brakes were fully mechanically operated, but the front brakes were 'push-rod' operated in order to utilize the considerable self-energization developed by the torsional effect of the brakes on the front axle assembly. The method was a phase in the development of the 'reversed action' front brakes used so effectively at Le Mans.

The first 6½ chassis (WB 2551) took the road in March, 1926; in frontal appearance it differed slightly from later models by reason of the absence of the casing carrying the engine-speed dynamo driven from the crankshaft, as the dynamo was camshaft-driven at the rear end of the engine.

In September, 1928, there were rumours afoot that there was every possibility that a 'Speed Model' of this chassis was scheduled for development and very early production. Much development work was, in fact, proceeding behind the scenes and culminated in the production of an entirely new type of chassis to be known as the 'Speed Six'.

The first of these chassis to be laid down was No. WT 2265, and the principal alterations in design were as follows:

High-compression pistons, giving 5·3 : 1 compression ratio.
Twin S.U. carburettors. BM 7032 camshaft. 0·019 tappet clearance.
'C'-type gearbox with indirect ratios—3rd, 1·357 to 1; 2nd, 1·823 to 1; 1st and reverse 3·364 to 1.
3·84 to 1 rear axle ratio.

The radiator was redesigned—the sides were parallel whereas the standard 6½ radiator had a pronounced taper inwards at the bottom—and the winged B had a green label.

From a commercial standpoint the 'Speed Six' development

had to include exploration of the probabilities and possibilities of this car superseding the now hard-pressed 4½ litre in the competition field. Intensive development work was carried out unobtrusively. Air-flow tests were made, the cylinder block was redesigned, port areas were altered, and brake endurance tests were carried out.

It is most interesting to read the report of Mr. Clarke on this chassis (LB 2332—see above) after winning the 1929 Le Mans:

(a) *During practice :* Slight steering instability reported and rectified by balancing the practice wheels and adjusting shock-dampers. Oil pressure—60 lbs.

(b) *During race :* Brake adjustment used up at the 20th hour.

(c) *After race* (Strip report).

Engine : Nothing to report. Exhaust valves and valve springs changed as a precautionary measure only.

Clutch : Nothing to report. Clutch-stop locating ears fractured.

Gearbox : Nothing to report. Mainshaft, first motion shaft and journal bearings changed as a precautionary measure.

Rear axle : Crown wheel and pinion—slight signs of pitting, otherwise O.K. Pinion thrust-race disintegrated. Otherwise O.K.

Brakes : Relined : two rear drums changed as a precautionary measure (local hot spot).

Frame : Small fracture through front engine-bearer engine-securing bolt hole. Signs of fracture where front wing stay palms connected to neutral section of frame channel due to 'fidgeting'.

Truly a remarkable strip report after a gruelling race of this calibre.

Altogether 544 6½-litre Bentleys were made, of which 171 were 'Speed Sixes' and of these, more than 70 are on the roads today in the hands of Bentley Drivers' Club members, including two of the team cars. GF 8507 (chassis No. HM 2868) is owned by J. D. Percy and is in its original form and beautifully kept. It was this car in which 'Babe' Barnato won Le Mans for the third time and, fittingly, it led his funeral cortège bearing floral tributes, driven by 'Babe's' chauffeur.

So concludes the story of truly one of the giants of the road, which never fails to impress wherever it appears. The majesty of the 'Speed Six' will continue for many years to dwarf motor-cars of younger vintage.

INDEX

Figures in bold type refer to the illustration facing the specified page. The Appendices are excluded from this index.

219